TIBETAN
SOUND HEALING

TENZIN WANGYAL RINPOCHE

TIBETAN
SOUND HEALING

Edited by Marcy Vaughn

SOUNDS TRUE
awakening wisdom

Sounds True, Inc.
Boulder CO 80306

© 2006 Tenzin Wangyal Rinpoche

Published 2006
Printed in Korea

ISBN-10: 1-59179-427-7
ISBN-13: 978-1-59179-427-1
Library of Congress Control Number 2006928850

TABLE OF CONTENTS

Preface

I WAS BORN in India to a very traditional Tibetan family. My mother and father both had fled Tibet with only the clothing on their backs. At a young age, I entered the monastery, where I received intensive training in the *Bön* Buddhist tradition. Bön is Tibet's most ancient spiritual tradition. It includes teachings and practices applicable to all parts of life, including our relationship with the elemental qualities of nature; our ethical and moral behavior; the development of love, compassion, joy, and equanimity; and Bön's highest teachings of *dzogchen,* or "great completion." According to the traditional Bön account of its origins, many thousands of years before the birth of the Buddha Shakyamuni in India, the Buddha Tonpa Shenrab Miwoche came to this world and expounded his teachings. Followers of Bön receive oral teachings and transmissions from teachers in a lineage unbroken from ancient times until the present day.

My monastic training included an eleven-year course of traditional studies at the Bön Dialectic School, culminating in a *geshe* degree, which could be considered the equivalent of a doctorate in the philosophy of religion in the West. While at the monastery, I lived closely with my teachers. One of my root teachers, Lopon Sangye Tenzin, recognized me as a *tulku,* or reincarnation, of the famous meditation master Khyungtul Rinpoche.

The Bön Buddhist tradition is a tradition rich with methods to guide all beings on the path to liberation. I am able to make these precious teachings available in the West because of the tireless dedication of my teachers to preserve these teachings and because of their profound wisdom and loving kindness.

Through teaching Western students, I have learned much. Tibetans are not used to asking so many questions! Many Western students helped me by asking questions about the *dharma,* the teachings about the path to liberation from suffering. In the challenge of bringing the Tibetan Bön Buddhist dharma to the West, these were very valuable questions. I had experienced one way of teaching in the monastery; I have experienced another way of teaching in the West. I come to the place of offering this practice of the Five Warrior Syllables as a result of my work, my practice, my interaction with students, and my interaction with Western culture. My teaching style is a result of many years of familiarity and reflection.

Dharma is not nearly as successful in the West as it can be, and this makes me sad. I see people doing all kinds of crazy things with Buddhist ideas and philosophy. For some, Buddhism is so intellectually stimulating that they discuss it for years. In the end, what is the result? What has changed in the student's conduct? Students repeat the same dharma discussions over and over with this teacher and then with a new teacher, with different students, and in different retreat situations. Afterward, many go back to exactly the same place where they began ten, fifteen, twenty years ago. The dharma has not deeply touched them or taken root in the proper way.

There is often a separation between the real issues that we live with in everyday life and the spiritual life to which we aspire. These two areas often don't communicate with each other at all. For example, in our spiritual practice we pray for the development of compassion by repeating, "May all sentient beings be free from suffering and the cause of suffering." But how real is compassion in your life? How deeply has that aspiration entered your life? If you investigate how you are actually living, you may be disappointed because you do not really feel compassion when you consider your annoying neighbor or your recent reaction to your aging parents. Even if you chant again and again, "May all sentient beings be free from suffering and the cause of suffering," someone who knows you very well could ask you, "When you say 'all sentient beings,' are you really including these five people, and especially that last one?"

This practice of the Five Warrior Syllables is a practice that can change your life. But you have to bring your spiritual practice into the very conditions and struggles of the life you are actually experiencing. If you cannot make changes in the simple struggles of your day-to-day life, then there is no way to make changes in the big places where you aspire to be of benefit to all beings. If you are not able to love someone with whom you live, or be kind to your parents, friends, and colleagues, then you cannot love strangers, and you certainly cannot love those who make you feel bad. Where do you begin? You begin with your own face. When you want to see changes in your life, and you don't see those changes, listen to the clear instructions of this meditation practice and bring the practice directly into your life.

It is my sincere desire that this simple and elegant practice of the Five Warrior Syllables, which is based on the highest teachings of the Tibetan Bön Buddhist tradition of which I am a lineage holder, will benefit many beings in the West. Please receive it with my blessing, and bring it into your life. Let it support you to become kind and strong and clear and awake.

Tenzin Wangyal Rinpoche
Charlottesville, Virginia
March 2006

Introduction

THE HEART OF the spiritual path is the longing to know and to be your true and authentic self. This has been the motivation of thousands who have gone before you and will come after you. According to the highest teachings in the Tibetan Bön Buddhist tradition, the true self that we long for is primordially pure. Each one of us, just as we are, is primordially pure. Of course when you hear that, you may think that it sounds like a great principle or philosophy, but you may not particularly feel that way right now. For your whole life, you have been flooded with images and messages that you are not pure, and it is easy for you to believe that you are not. Nevertheless, according to the teachings, your true nature is pure. That is who you really are.

Why is it so difficult to access or experience this purity? Why is there so much confusion and suffering? The truth of the matter is that our true self is too close to the mind that experiences suffering. It is so close we rarely recognize it, and so it is obscured. The good news is that the moment we begin to suffer or recognize that we are confused, we have an opportunity to awaken. Suffering shakes us and brings us the opportunity to awaken to a deeper truth. Most of the time when we suffer, we feel we need to change something in order to improve our lives. We change our jobs, relationships, diet, personal habits, and on and on. There are huge industries driven by this restless need that we experience to constantly improve our conditions and ourselves. While these actions may provide temporary relief or improve the quality of life, the methods never seem to go deep enough to cut the root of our dissatisfaction. This simply means that through all the methods of self-improvement we engage, as beneficial as they may seem, we have not fully met and become who we truly are.

Our dissatisfaction is useful when it makes us ask new questions, but it is most helpful when we ask the *right* question. According to the highest teaching in my tradition, the question we should be asking is, "Who is suffering? Who is experiencing this problem?" This a very important question to ask, but if it is not asked in the right way, it is possible to end up with the wrong conclusion. When we ask, "Who is suffering?" we have to look directly and clearly into the inner space of our being. Many do not look long enough or thoroughly enough to connect with their innermost essence.

Encountering dissatisfaction is a necessary motivation on the spiritual path. Bringing it directly into your meditation practice, it becomes a powerful entrance to connecting with the pure space of being. Working with the Five Warrior Syllables as a meditation practice, you do connect with your primordially pure self. Having connected, you can develop trust and confidence in that authentic self, and your life can reflect and express the spontaneous and virtuous actions that arise from this authentic and true self.

OVERVIEW OF THE FIVE WARRIOR SYLLABLES

Our fundamental awake nature is not produced or created, but is already there. In the way the vast expanse of the sky is present but may be obscured by clouds, we too are obscured by habitual patterns that we mistake for ourselves. The practice of the Five Warrior Syllables is a skillful means that can support us to release our negative and limiting behavioral patterns of body, speech, and mind, and make room for a more spontaneous, creative, and authentic expression. In this practice, we recognize, connect with, and trust what is already there. In a relative sense, we begin to practice loving kindness, compassion, joy, and equanimity, qualities that bring great benefit experienced and expressed in our relationship with self and others. Ultimately, the practice brings us to the full recognition of our true self. In the teachings, the metaphor for this experience is a child recognizing her mother in a crowd—an instant, deep recognition of connection, an experience of home. This is referred to as the natural mind, and that mind is pure. In the natural mind, all virtues are spontaneously perfected.

There are many different ways we can practice meditation and connect with our true self. In my book on the five elements, *Healing with Form, Energy, and Light,* I talk about using the power of the natural world to support a deeper and more authentic connection with our essence. When we stand on top of a mountain, we get an unquestionable experience of vast and open space. It is important to realize that that feeling, that experience, is in us and not only in the impressive vista. With a mountain, we can connect with and develop stability. Many of us go to the ocean for rest and enjoyment, but the natural power of the ocean can support us to develop openness. We can go into nature to connect with certain qualities and internalize those qualities, in the sense of taking what we feel in the physical connection and bringing that deeper inside where our experience becomes one of energy and mind.

Many times we look at a flower and think, "So beautiful! So beautiful!" At that moment, it is good to realize that beautiful quality internally. Feel it with the support of looking at the flower. Don't merely look at the flower or any external object and conclude that the beauty rests there in that object. Then you are only seeing your belief that the flower is beautiful but has nothing to do with you. Bring that quality and feeling to a deeper recognition: "I am experiencing this. The flower is supporting me to experience this." Rather than, "It's just a flower. I'm not like that." We have so many opportunities to try this in life.

In the practice of the Five Warrior Syllables, we are not coming from the outside in. The approach here is from a discovery of internal space and moving from there to spontaneous manifestation. With sound, we clear our habitual tendencies and obstacles and connect with the clear and open space of our being. This open space is the source of all virtues and is fundamental to each of us. It is simply who we are—awake, clear, buddha.

There are five warrior syllables—*A, OM, HUNG, RAM,* and *DZA*—and each syllable represents a quality of realization. They are referred to as "seed syllables" because they possess the *essence* of enlightenment. These five syllables represent the body, speech, mind, virtuous qualities, and actions of enlightenment, respectively. Together, they represent the true and fully expressed nature of our authentic self.

In the practice, we sing each warrior syllable in sequence. With each syllable, we focus on a corresponding energy center, or *chakra,* in the body and connect with the quality that corresponds with that syllable. The sequence moves from the pure open space of being to the place of the manifestation of virtue in action. As you begin each practice session, you come as your ordinary self, bringing those conditions and patterns of your life that you are seeking to open, clear, and transform—both those of which you are aware and those that are hidden from you. The first point of focus is the forehead chakra. A chakra is simply an energetic location in the body, similar to a wheel or center where many energy pathways converge. These centers are not at the surface of the body but are within the body along the central channel, a channel of light that extends from below the navel straight up through the center of the body and opens at the crown. Different systems of practice use different chakras as focal points. In the Five Warrior Syllables practice, *A* is associated with the forehead chakra and the changeless body; *OM* with the throat and the quality of unceasing speech; *HUNG* with the heart and the quality of undeluded mind; *RAM* with the navel chakra and ripened, virtuous qualities; and *DZA* with the secret chakra and spontaneous action.

Pronunciation Guide

ཨ   *A* ~ pronounced "ah" like the "a" sound in the word *calm*

ༀ   *OM* ~ rhymes with the word *home*

ཧཱུྃ   *HUNG* ~ the "u" sounds like the "oo" in the word *hook*

རཾ   *RAM* ~ the "a" sounds like the "a" in the word *calm*

ཛ   *DZA* ~ sharp and percussive; the front upper and lower teeth come together, with the tongue pressing against them as you sharply release the "dz" sound into the "ah" sound like the "a" in the word *calm*

By simply drawing our attention to a chakra location, subtle *prana* is activated. Prana is the Sanskrit word for "vital breath"; the Tibetan word is *lung,* while the Chinese use *qi* or *chi,* and the Japanese, *ki.* I refer to connection with this level of experience as the energetic dimension. Through the vibration of the sound of the particular syllable, we activate the possibility of dissipating physical, emotional or energetic, and mental disturbances that are held in the prana, or vital breath. As we bring mind, breath, and sound vibration together, we can begin to feel shifts and changes at the levels of our body, emotions, and mind. Through releasing blocks and then recognizing and resting in the space within us that clears and opens, we enter a higher state of consciousness.

Each seed syllable has a corresponding quality of light, a particular color. *A* is white, *OM* is red, *HUNG* is blue, *RAM* is red, and *DZA* is green. When we sing the syllable, we also visualize or imagine the light radiating from the chakra. This supports us to dissipate the subtlest obscurations of mind and to experience the natural radiance of the awakened mind.

Through the powerful combination of focus on a particular location, the vibration of the sound, and the awareness of light, we develop an increasingly clear and open presence, radiant with positive qualities. The qualities themselves, among them love, compassion, joy, and equanimity, become supports or entrances to an even deeper connection with self, a deeper wisdom, the very space from which all of existence arises.

In the practice of the Five Warrior Syllables, we have a departing place, the place of conditions and dissatisfactions; a few doorways through which to enter, which are the chakras; and a final destination, our essential being.

OUTER, INNER, AND SECRET LEVELS OF EXPERIENCE

These syllables are referred to as warrior syllables. The term *warrior* refers to the ability to conquer the forces of negativity. Sacred sound has the power to eliminate obstacles, emotional blocks, and mental obscurations that prevent us from recognizing the nature of mind and from being our authentic self in any given moment. We can look at obstacles on three levels: external, internal, and secret. External obstacles are sickness and other adverse circumstances. Whatever the external causes and conditions, the Five Warrior Syllables practice is a means to work with and overcome the suffering we experience in relation to those conditions. Through the practice, we also eliminate internal obstacles, which are the negative emotions such as ignorance, anger, attachment, jealousy, and pride. And through this practice, the secret obstacles of doubt, hope, and fear can be overcome.

Even when external situations are the strongest obstacles in your life, you ultimately have to deal with them yourself, by yourself, with yourself. When you overcome such obstacles, you are still left with the question, "How is it that I continually find myself in situations like this? Where do all these active negative emotions come from?" Even if it seems the outer world has turned against you, or a particular person is making trouble for you, somehow it has something to do with you. Perhaps you are aware of the many emotions, needs, and conditions within yourself. Where these needs and conditions and emotions originate is a much deeper place in yourself than you may realize, so we need a method that allows us to connect deeply and intimately with ourselves, a method that brings the powerful remedy of clear and open awareness to the root of our suffering and confusion.

Ordinarily, we recognize a problem only when it becomes a gross problem. When problems are very subtle, we are not able to recognize them. I don't imagine that there are many conversations happening at the local coffee shop that begin, "I have a real problem in my life because I have fundamental ignorance and tend to impute myself as solid and substantial." Or, "I have a lot of problems in my life. I am continuously engaging the five poisons." You are more likely to hear, "I'm not doing very well. My partner and I are fighting."

When problems manifest in your outer life, you can't miss them. When you experience them, you may even recognize that you are participating in creating them. But the seeds of these problems are very hard to recognize and would be considered a secret obstacle. The notion of "secret" simply means that it is harder to understand; it is hidden from us.

What is your secret problem? Usually you have to wait until your secret problem ripens and becomes your inner problem; then, when your inner problem ripens, it becomes your outer problem. When it becomes your outer problem, you share it with all your family and friends! When it is inner or secret, you don't share it with anyone. Others may have no idea that you are experiencing a problem. You may have no idea. But when it becomes an outer problem, even when you don't want to share it, you have involved others in it.

If you look at the nature of the problem, when something manifests in the outer world, clearly it is an outer obstacle. But when you see who created it, what kind of emotion or condition created it, you may recognize, "My greed has created this condition." Looking and working at the level of the greed is working with the inner level of obstacle. "Who is so greedy?" points to the secret level. So "Who is so greedy?" becomes the secret obscuration, the greed becomes the inner emotional block, and the expression of greed in the outer world—whatever problems you create—become the outer obstacles.

What do these obstacles, blocks, and obscurations obscure? On the secret level, they obscure wisdom. On the inner level, they obscure virtues. In outer manifestation, they obscure the expression of virtue toward others. When these obstacles, blocks, and obscurations are removed, wisdom, the virtuous qualities, and the spontaneous expression of those virtues are naturally present.

On the most subtle or secret level of being, each of the five warrior syllables reveals a corresponding wisdom: the wisdom of emptiness, mirrorlike wisdom, the wisdom of equanimity, discriminating-awareness wisdom, and the wisdom of all-accomplishing action. On the inner level, positive qualities are revealed. I refer to love, compassion, joy, and equanimity as "enlightened qualities." They are also known as the Four Immeasurables. While there are innumerable positive qualities, for the purpose of this practice, I encourage you to develop a deeper relation to these four. Everyone needs these qualities; we are more aware of a need for virtuous qualities than for wisdom. Through connecting with these inner qualities, we can connect with a deeper source of wisdom in ourselves and also benefit others through the outer expression of these positive qualities in our actions.

While we recognize the need for love, compassion, joy, and equanimity in our lives, instead of connecting with these qualities by looking inward, we often connect our need for them with material objects. For one person, love may mean finding a partner. Joy might mean getting a house or a job or new clothing or a particular car. We often experience our needs as materially based. "I need to find something in order to be happy." We seek to acquire or accumulate these virtues in a material sense. But with the support of our meditation practice, we begin to look inward and discover a more fundamental place within us in which all these qualities are already present.

In the beginning of our practice, the Four Immeasurables can be approached in a mundane way. This is what is real for each of us, and we have to acknowledge this as our starting point. We begin with the very basic conditions of our lives. You may recognize that you are irritable around your colleagues at work or have lost a sense of delight in your children. If you understand your very basic conditions and bring them to the practice, you can make those basic conditions the bridge to discovering the positive qualities within you. The qualities then become the bridge to wisdom. There is always a place to grow in this practice. You should not think, "Oh, I found my soul mate, someone to love; that is my illumination." Your practice doesn't finish there. At the same time, you do want to see the positive results of your meditation manifesting in your relationships and in your creative expression.

So we begin the practice of meditation more familiar with our suffering and confusion than with the purity of our being. The problems that we bring are the energy or fuel that will power our path. The clearing of our blocks through engaging the power of the Five Warrior Syllables offers us the opportunity to glimpse the open sky of our being. The dissolution of these blockages reveals wisdom and makes positive qualities available. This is the warrior's path. The spontaneous expression of positive qualities and virtues in our lives is the direct result of meditation, as is the confidence that naturally arises as we become more and more familiar with our true nature.

SHORT-TERM AND LONG-TERM GOALS IN MEDITATION

When we engage in the practice of meditation, I recommend having some immediate goals as well as understanding the ultimate or long-term goal. While the long-term goal of the practice of meditation is to cut the root of ignorance and achieve liberation or buddhahood for the benefit of all beings, the immediate goal can be something more ordinary. What is it that you want to transform in your life? A short-term goal may range from overcoming a basic condition of suffering in your life to cultivating positive, healing qualities that benefit yourself, your family, and your community.

You can begin your meditation practice in a very simple place. Reflect on your life to see what it is that you would like to transform. I recommend working with a personal issue in this practice of the Five Warrior Syllables. Let's say you are unhappy in life. Every now and then you think, "I have a lot of reasons to be happy; I should just focus on those things." So you focus your thoughts in a more positive direction, and it works for a couple of hours or for the weekend. Somehow, by the middle of next week, you're back to the more familiar feeling of being unhappy. Perhaps you have a cup of tea and talk to someone. It helps for a few hours, but again, you're back. Or you go to a therapist, and that also helps, but still you go back to a familiar feeling of unhappiness. Somehow you get trapped back in a pattern that you find difficult to overcome completely. Somehow your unhappiness is deeper within you than the methods you have tried. It is possible to connect with an experience of yourself that is more fundamental than any of the problems you experience in life, to recognize this again and again through the practice of meditation, and to trust this experience of being. Through singing the warrior syllables and recognizing, becoming familiar with, and resting in the inner space that opens up within you as a result, you begin to trust a more fundamental place within yourself that is not only clear and open and free of problems, but from which all positive qualities are spontaneously available as you encounter the challenges of your life.

USING THIS BOOK AND CD

In the following five chapters, I will describe each of the warrior syllables and how we might practice with them in order to benefit ourselves and others. After reading each chapter, you may wish to pause, and listen to and practice along with the track on the CD that is the short guided meditation corresponding to the syllable described. In this way, you can become more familiar with that particular syllable and bring what you have been reading and reflecting upon directly into your experience in a deeper way. This is the traditional Buddhist way of progressing on the path: reading or hearing the teaching, reflecting upon what you have read or heard, and then bringing what you have understood directly into your meditation practice. The final track of the CD is the complete meditation of the Five Warrior Syllables.

I have included a chapter on establishing an ongoing meditation practice, and finally I include a script of a guided meditation similar to the guided instruction on the CD that accompanies this book. In the Appendix are instructions for the *tsa lung* exercises, which I strongly recommend learning and practicing. In your daily life, I suggest that you begin each session of meditation with these five tsa lung exercises. They will help you to open and clear obstacles, blocks, and obscurations to abiding in meditation.

CHAPTER
ONE

The First Syllable: A

Sing again and again the self-originated sound of A.
Radiate luminous white light from the forehead chakra.
The secret karmic obscurations dissolve at the source,
Clear and open like a cloudless desert sky.
Abide without changing or elaborating.
All fears are overcome
And changeless confidence is attained.
May I experience the wisdom of emptiness.

SPACE PERVADES EVERY aspect of the body and every aspect of the environment. Space is fundamental to all matter, to every human being, to the whole physical universe. Because of this, we can speak of space as the base or ground within which all the other elements play and out of which both our familiar problematic world and our enlightened sacred world manifest.

According to the dzogchen teachings, the highest teachings in the Bön Buddhist tradition, space is the very ground of our being. As such, it is changeless. This dimension of being is primordially pure. It is referred to as the wisdom body of all the buddhas, the dimension of truth, or *dharmakaya.*

To recognize our open and pure being, we first connect with space. Deeply connecting with ourselves is always a question of connecting with space. The quality of space is openness. It takes time to recognize and become familiar with the open space of being. On the level of the body, that pure space may be occupied by disease or pain. Energetically, that space may be occupied by emotional blockages. In our minds, that space may be occupied by obscurations such as doubt or the constant traffic of thoughts.

The sound of *A* is described as self-arising sound, pure sound. According to the teachings of dzogchen, the use of sound practice is not so much about the quality of the sound, but rather about the essence. When we produce sound, some level of awareness stays in that sound. So as we sing *A* again and again, we listen to the sound. It is like practicing with the breath. We are focusing on the breath; breath is us; breath is our life; breath is our life force; breath is our soul. Sound cannot be produced unless we breathe. The breath and the sound are so close to each other. So when we are producing sound, we are relating to the breath and vibration of the sound itself. In a sense it is very pure—the producer is the listener; the listener is the producer. In this way, we can experience the sound as self-arising.

When you make the sound *A*, the sound *A* has a mind aspect and a breath or body aspect. When you breathe and you bring your awareness to that breath, then the mind and breath come together. In the Tibetan tradition, we say that the mind is like a rider and the horse is the breath. The path the horse follows in this practice will be the chakra locations of the body, and the armor or protection that the rider wears will be the warrior seed syllables. This armor protects the rider—the mind of awareness—from falling into hope and fear and following the discursive thinking mind that tries to manage our experience.

When you sing *A* again and again, through the power and protection and vibration of *A*, the mind rides the prana, or breath, in the sound; and the physical, emotional, and subtle obstacles to recognizing yourself as changeless are cleared. This means that an outcome of the practice of the sound of *A* will be that, deep inside, you open. You feel it. If you do it properly, you will feel that openness. The moment you feel yourself open, that is a great success. You have found the ground, which we call the ground of all: the base, which we call *kunzhi*, which is openness.

When you sing *A*, bring your focus to the forehead chakra and sing the sound very clearly. The first level of connection is with the physical sound. Next, feel a connection with the energy or vibration of that sound. Visualize white light radiating from your forehead chakra to support the most subtle dimension of being. *A* represents space, the eternal body, the changeless body. The moment we sing *A*, we want to feel or connect with openness and spaciousness. Through the vibration of *A*, we become aware of and release whatever blocks us, and through the dissolution of the blocks, we are gradually opening, opening, opening, opening, opening, opening. Deep obscurations get released. When release occurs, some sense of inner space begins to open up. The effect of *A* will develop as you continue to practice.

A supports you to recognize the changeless state of awareness and being. The analogy is a clear desert sky with no clouds. Whatever occupies you, whether it is sadness or agitation or a busy mind, is like clouds. Through sound and vibration and awareness, the clouds gradually dissipate and the open sky is revealed. Whenever the emotion, obstacle, or obscuration begins to release, it opens the space. It is simply the experience of openness. What happens if you remove objects from a table? The space opens. Then you can place a vase of flowers on the table. So what does *A* do? It clears. It cleans. It opens up the space.

It is important to know that we are not creating space or developing or improving ourselves in this practice. At some point in our experience, space simply opens and we recognize what is already there—the pure open space of being. At this point, the instruction is to abide, without changing or elaborating. This is the dzogchen view. This is what is taught in the highest teaching. Meditation is the process of becoming familiar with openness. So in this practice, we try to feel the sound, the energy of the sound, and the space of the sound. When you connect with the space, you abide or rest there.

Perhaps you don't feel that any particular thing is obscuring you as you begin the practice. There is always something obscuring you, but you may not be aware of it. Simply sing *A* again and again, and then rest in open awareness. Alternatively, you may be aware of a disturbance or a block, so feel the vibration of the sound *A* as you sing, and feel the sound dissipating the block that you bring into your consciousness. The vibration of *A* is like a weapon that cuts duality, cuts the back-and-forth journey of your discursive mind, cuts your doubts, hesitations, and lack of clarity. Whatever obscures openness begins to shake and dissipate into the space, and as it dissipates, you become clearer and clearer. You connect to the clear space because the energy and emotion that you brought to consciousness has transformed. When the block dissipates, you feel some space. That space is something you want to recognize. You want to recognize and rest in that space without changing. That is the introduction to openness, to the boundless space of being. By bringing your dissatisfaction directly into the practice and sounding *A* again and again, the energy of that dissatisfaction can dissolve and, through that dissolution, introduce you to the clear and open space of your being.

You might ask, "What does releasing my fear or my anger have to do with a higher sense of the dzogchen view of abiding in openness, abiding in the nature of mind?" If your main goal is to be happy and free of a particular problem in your life, perhaps your goal is not to abide without changing in the nature of mind. You don't know what it means to abide without changing. Your wish and intention is simply to not be bothered by your fear or anger, so the immediate goal of your meditation is to overcome that. In many, many tantric teachings it is said, "When desire manifests, turn the desire into a path. When anger manifests, turn anger into a path." With any negative emotion, obstacle, or problem—no matter how personal it seems—your problem can become your path. This is what is taught. It means that you can enter into higher realization directly through your problem.

This is not the usual approach. Usually what happens is that when anger manifests, it creates a problem in your life. It drives your reactions; it results in unkind or harsh words. You go too far with it, and it hurts you and hurts others. Instead of letting anger begin to destroy, use it as a path. That is what we are doing with this practice. So each time you begin your practice, bring to mind whatever issue in your life you want to transform. Look at it and say, "You are my path. I am going to transform you into my path. This situation is going to help me to grow." And absolutely, that is the case.

As you begin a session of meditation practice, it is important to feel the block; locate it in your body, in your emotions, or in your mind. Try to get as close as possible to the direct experience of this obscuration. Let's take an example from ordinary life: "I'm afraid to be in a committed relationship." You can approach this analytically and examine possible causes for your fear. Perhaps your first relationship was overwhelming and you needed to end it, and in the process you hurt the other person. You are always affected in some way by the consequences of your actions. But in this practice, we are not analyzing our actions and their consequences. That isn't to say that analyzing has no value; it is simply not our approach. Here, the approach is very simple. Feel your fear because you have produced it. It has ripened. We are not thinking about how it ripened. Rather, we are connecting directly with the experience of this fear in the body, in the prana, and in the mind. Bring this fear vividly to awareness. Again, this is not about thinking or analyzing a problem, but simply about encountering it directly as experience in this very moment.

Then, sing *A* again and again. Allow the vibration of the sacred sound to work. With the sound, you are clearing, clearing, clearing. Something happens. There is some release. Even if there is only a small release, that is fine. When you sing *A* and when you clear, a little window opens up, a space. In all these clouds, you see a little hole. Perhaps you have never experienced that little hole. Through that little hole, you glimpse clear sky. It is very small, but it is clear sky. Our ordinary experience of *A* will be a glimpse of openness, a clearing. The infinite and boundless sky exists beyond those clouds, and you see a glimpse of that. That is your door. When you are practicing with *A*, when you feel a moment of openness, that is your door. You can change your habitual position of sitting on a big cushion of dark clouds, because you can see the dark clouds, and you see a little hole appearing. The moment you see the space, draw your attention there. That means you are changing your seat. The moment you see that glimpse of space is the beginning of becoming more familiar with that space. You don't want to see the space and be distracted. You just want to stay in the experience of the space. The more you remain without changing anything, the more the space opens; the more you remain, the more it opens; the more you remain, the more it opens.

Once these clouds clear, the foundation upon which you are resting is somewhere you have never rested before. Open space is the foundation. Something has released, and in the space that opens, you sit without changing. Recognize that space as mother, as buddha, as the most sacred space you can ever discover within yourself. Recognize that space as a doorway to the totality of being. The special experience of *A* is abiding in emptiness. Through the recognition of this sacred space within yourself, you receive the empowerment of the dharmakaya, the wisdom body of all the buddhas, the dimension of truth. This is the highest result that the practice brings.

So, going back to the practice, you work with *A*. Once *A* clears some obscuration, it opens up that space. That is very important. It opens up that space. Then, abide without changing. So you bring your pain or dissatisfaction or anger to the practice, sing the syllable *A* again and again, dissolve the obscuration, and rest in the space that has opened up. Many times people have no good idea about why they should rest in that space. That space is not all that exciting. It is very common to want to get rid of something. Everyone is interested in getting rid of something. "I want to get rid of sadness. I don't want to be unhappy." But once some space releases or opens in the meditation, because that space is not familiar or exciting, there may be a tendency to look for the next problem.

I am emphasizing here that this is your moment to enter the experience of the primordial purity of being. You enter through your own personal experience. That is the most powerful way of entering. When you do that, you experience two benefits. First, you develop a very clear recognition of what abiding, or resting without changing, means. Second, when you have a clear recognition of what abiding means, you have a powerful means of overcoming inner obstacles. The obstacles have changed. You cannot really abide unless they have changed, and you cannot change them unless you abide. So these two things are interrelated.

Once you glimpse openness in the practice and can abide there, you have the opportunity to experience wisdom. There is a particular wisdom connected with each of the five syllables. With *A*, the wisdom is referred to as the wisdom of emptiness. You have the opportunity to experience the wisdom of emptiness or something close to it. Why? Because of your obscuration. Your obscuration actually helps you. Probably you will not be able to experience the wisdom of emptiness, you will not be able to abide in a clear space, unless you experience that obscuration. Therefore, your obscuration becomes a path, a very important means to enter the wisdom of emptiness.

With the sound of *A*, we clear blockages in order to discover the ground of our being as changeless. *A* supports us to recognize and rest in our changeless being. *A* represents the changeless body of all the buddhas. As you read this, perhaps you think to yourself, "Okay, *A* means changeless." But if you look at your experience, what you may notice is that everything is constantly changing. Your experience is completely the opposite of the description of *A!* You have a body that is constantly changing, and your thoughts are changing faster than your body. But if we can look directly at our being, in the middle of all this change is the changeless dimension. We are trying to connect with that changeless dimension through this practice. Of course, trying to connect is not the same as connecting, because trying is just another version of change! And through our thinking process, we can go on and on and on. So stop. Stop talking to yourself. Stop following your thoughts. Be. Rest. Discover more space inside yourself. The direction you are going is to discover more space in yourself. You are not trying to activate more and more thinking. Create an environment and a focus that contributes to discovering that sense of changeless being. Find a comfortable posture and then apply the method of *A*.

The confidence that develops through success in the practice of *A* is called "changeless confidence." Your very perception of your being can be affected by this practice to the point that even when changes occur, you don't change. You have discovered the stability of open awareness, the confidence of the changeless body. The best way to develop confidence is to clear whatever blocks or obscures you from the direct experience of the open and clear sky of being. What may begin as an idea, then a momentary glimpse of experience, gradually ripens with familiarity. Changeless confidence comes with some degree of ripeness in the experience of openness. Openness becomes trustworthy. The development of confidence is not so much a matter of doing anything, but as you continue to connect with openness in your practice, and as you rest and abide in openness more and more, changeless confidence will be a natural result.

So this is our practice. We approach the highest level of dharma with the lowest level of problem. We begin with a very specific awareness of a situation of life we wish to transform, a direct and intimate sense of our confusion, and we transform that condition into our path through the method of singing *A*—through our direct experience in this moment. Through the power of the sacred sound, we glimpse an opening, and through recognizing this opening as the pure and fundamental ground of our being, we abide there without changing: open, clear, awake, confident.

LISTEN TO TRACK 1
The First Syllable: *A*

CHAPTER
TWO

The Second Syllable: OM

Sing again and again the self-clear sound of OM.
Radiate luminous red light from the throat chakra.
All knowledge and experiences of the Four Immeasurables
Arise like sunshine in the clear, cloudless sky.
Abiding there: clear, radiant, complete,
All conditions of hope are overcome
And ceaseless confidence is attained.
May I experience mirrorlike wisdom.

AS *A* CONNECTS us with the space of being, *OM* connects us with awareness, or light, within that space. Once you are able to feel a connection with internal space, that experience of openness naturally provides a sense of completeness.

The inner space that opens up is not an empty space, but is a space of full-ness and aliveness and awareness, which can be experienced as a sense of feeling complete. Usually our sense of completeness or satisfaction is conditional. "I feel so good because I finally fixed my car today." "I feel great because it is such a gorgeous day!" These are conventional, changeable reasons to experience satis-faction. It is fine to feel satisfaction, but it is important not to be dependent on external things that cause us to feel complete, because they are impermanent.

There may be times when you feel complete deep inside with few reasons. Other times, you have so many reasons for feeling that way: you have a new job, your relationship is going well, you are enjoying good health. Whatever reasons you have for feeling complete, they involve subtle and constant hope. There is always an edge or a shadow to your feeling of completeness in any given moment. "I'm doing well, as long as I keep this job," or "I feel great," you say, smiling. And the shadow text is, "I feel great, and I want you to be with me all the time," or "I'm happy as long as I have my good health." This is our subcon-scious dialogue subverting our state of being. Somehow we are always on the edge. Our completeness is always on the edge.

The sound *OM* is self-clear. This means that clarity is not produced by any cause or condition but that the space of our being is clear in itself. *OM* repre-sents this clarity. Through the vibration of *OM*, we clear all our conditions and reasons for feeling complete. We penetrate all our causes and conditions until we feel some sense of completeness without a reason. With this practice, we explore what completeness without a reason feels like.

When you sing the syllable, you may feel a certain pleasure of releasing some-thing. After you release, you may feel a bit lost or disoriented. You may not know what to do because the space is less familiar to you than the thoughts or feelings or sensations that previously occupied it. The instruction in the meditation is to recognize space and rest there, and because of this encouragement, you may rest deeply enough to have a little glimpse of light. Wow! You experience "Wow!" because light spontaneously comes from that space. Why does light spontaneously arise from that space? Because space is open. The light that pervades that openness is the light of our awareness. We experience light as vividness and clarity and energy.

At this point, it is possible to allow the infinite potential of awareness to be experienced directly. Instead, what often happens first is that your relationship is to the experience of releasing. You are so tired of being sad or confused or angry, and yet once you release that emotion, you are perhaps a bit lost. If you are too lost, you will not recognize and allow the experience of *OM*. You might open but then shut down quickly again and miss the possibility of experiencing clear and vivid awareness.

Following the progression of this practice of the Five Warrior Syllables, when inner space opens up, what happens? We allow experience. We allow ourselves to experience ourselves fully. We allow the experience of the whole world fully in that space. The potential is there to experience everything in its fullness. But we often don't allow that fullness, because the moment we have a little openness, we have fear. We don't recognize the openness for what it is. We shut down immediately. The way we shut down is by occupying that space. That is where loneliness and isolation begin. Somehow we cannot manage to recognize ourselves or connect deeply with ourselves in that space. Space has to be occupied immediately or we are uncomfortable. Often people get depressed after the loss of a husband, wife, or friend, because the people with whom they are truly connected become the representation of the light and the vividness in life. When their loved ones are gone, they feel that the light is gone. They have experienced the light in others, rather than in the space itself. They did not recognize the light within themselves fully.

When we draw our attention to our throat and sing *OM*, we feel not only open, but in that openness, we feel fully alive. In our human experience, when we are open and feel fully alive, we feel complete. Most of us are not familiar with feeling complete experiencing space and light. We know how to feel complete experiencing others or things. Feeling complete experiencing space and light is what we are trying to become familiar with through the practice of *OM*. Often we do not recognize ourselves as complete in this moment. So bring to the practice of *OM* any feelings of lack or incompleteness or emptiness that you may experience. Feel directly your body, emotions, and patterns of thought. As you feel them directly, without analyzing, sing *OM* again and again, and allow the power of the vibration of *OM* to dissipate and dissolve those patterns that hold the experience of lack or incompleteness. As you experience release and opening, imagine that the red light in the throat chakra supports your openness and awareness. Then rest in the vividness of the awareness of each moment.

When you feel completely open, you feel full. Nothing is missing; nothing is lacking. In the practice, when you have the experience of boundless space, that space is not empty or dead. Space is complete. Space is full of potentiality, light, awareness. The metaphor for this is the sun shining in the cloudless sky. The light of our awareness pervades our experience of openness. In that space there is light. There is awareness in our openness, and that awareness is light.

As you sing *OM*, feel the space and feel the light. Through the practice, develop familiarity with this. Encourage the experience: "I am complete as I am." As *A* connects us with the space of being, *OM* connects us with the light within that space. The sun is shining in the cloudless sky. The space of our being is not empty at all, but is full of light, complete with the light of awareness, the unceasing light of our wakefulness, the natural radiance of wisdom mind.

The seed syllable *OM* connects us with mirrorlike wisdom. How can we understand mirrorlike wisdom? When you look beautiful and stand before a mirror, the mirror does not comment, "No, this mirror is only for people who have something to fix." When your hair is a mess, the mirror does not say, "Yes, welcome to the club. I'm here to help." No, the mirror doesn't comment. The mirror has nothing to do with what gender you are, what color you are, or how tired or rested you look. The mirror is clear and reflects what is.

Mirrorlike wisdom is the awareness that recognizes appearance as a mirror does—without judgment. Whatever arises is clear, vivid, present, and does not affect the primordial purity of your mind. Consider the mirror in an airport bathroom. Does the mirror ever say, "I am tired of all these people coming in looking exhausted? Just look at these people!" By contrast, doctors, teachers, people who relate to numbers of people each day, do become affected by the people they see and have less and less mirrorlike wisdom as the day progresses. The world affects us. Perhaps you get affected too often or too easily. You can become so vulnerable that life is very difficult. As it becomes more and more difficult, you have less access to mirrorlike wisdom. If somebody talks to you, it affects you. If somebody doesn't talk to you, it affects you. Almost everything affects you. As you sing *OM* again and again, you release blocks to your awareness and connect with the clear light of your natural mind. With *A*, you abide in the changeless experience. With *OM*, you abide in clarity. You abide in awareness.

At this point in the practice, you are paying attention to the sun shining in the sky. The space is not only open, but there is pure energy in that space. The sacred syllable *OM* represents the unceasing speech of all enlightened beings. Unceasing means infinite; it is endlessly arising movement, energy, awareness, luminosity.

The nature of mind is clear. In every given moment, if even the most confused mind knows how to look at itself directly, it finds that the nature of mind itself is always clear. The mind at that very moment may appear beset by waves of emotions, but the nature of mind itself is always clear. Delusion is not there. Delusion *appears.* If appearance is everything for you, then you are deluded. If the base or foundation of space is more important than its ever-changing appearance, then you are not deluded.

Now that the space is clear with *OM,* you abide in this space, feeling a sense of its completeness. Try not to interfere with that sense of completeness through logic and reason. You are simply complete. Try to stay with that sense of completeness with no reason.

OM means infinite, unlimited positive qualities. If these qualities can be brought down to a single idea, that idea would be compassion. As I said, space is not empty in the sense of lacking; the nature of space is compassion. In that sense, space is full and complete. Buddhism describes wisdom and compassion as the two wings of a bird. In order for a bird to fly, two wings are necessary. In order to complete the journey of awakening, you must recognize the fullness of space. Wisdom is the *A,* the space. Compassion is the *OM,* the quality. If we describe only one positive quality, that quality is compassion. Qualities of mind are infinite, however. For instance, there are the Four Immeasurables—love, compassion, joy, and equanimity. We can name many other positive qualities, such as generosity, clarity, openness, and peacefulness. It is traditionally stated that there are 84,000 positive qualities of mind.

All these positive qualities, all this beauty, all this perfection is within us. The reason we don't realize these qualities in any given moment is because our connection with the open space is blocked. That's where the practice of *A* supports us. If space is not there, the qualities will not manifest. So space is fundamental. In the material world, space is very important for creating a lighting system. An architect needs the right space to achieve the right light. You may desire a lot of light, but in the wrong space, light is not going to manifest. If you have a lot of space, many positive qualities will manifest. In our personal experience, whether or not we experience these positive qualities within ourselves will depend on our connection with or realization of space.

There are so many different psychological techniques and therapies and healing modalities employed today. With most of them, the method is based on the creation of thoughts. You create ideas, meaning, and understanding based on thinking. That is not the approach here. Here, we are discovering a foundation. If there is space, there is light. Further, if there is light, there is the union of the light and space—there is a radiant manifestation. These radiant manifestations are not thoughts or the product of thoughts. It is not that I am happy because I have a car. I am just happy because of the space and light. So rather than improving or clarifying our thoughts, we are accessing a more fundamental place in our being.

In the conventional world, we seek happiness. Will abiding without changing and abiding in this luminous space support you to be happier in your work? Yes. If you do not have confidence in this yet, you have to trust a little bit, take a small leap of faith, and try the practice. You don't have anything to lose. You can say, "Well, you made me rest another hour in the nature of mind, and nothing happened!" And perhaps your inner smile didn't come because you have so much work to do in the office. But the possibility is there, and with further practice, you can experience positive results.

We overcome fear with *A. OM* overcomes hope. Fear is related to space. Hope is related to clarity. Hope comes because of some sense of lack of perfection.

When you sing *OM* again and again, try to feel that everything is perfected. "I'm complete." These are the simple words: "I am complete as I am." Begin to meditate on feeling a sense of completeness. Naturally, you will feel less and less need or hope for anything else. In this way, it is possible to overcome the condition of hope. We all need some kind of hope in life, but sometimes when we hope too much, hope itself becomes our primary suffering.

In the open space of our being, love, compassion, joy, and equanimity are ceaselessly perfected. This means that they arise instantly and spontaneously. These and other enlightened qualities are not ceaselessly perfected in "conditioned" space. Conditioned space is present when you are so caught up with your thoughts and emotions that your mind is not open. As a result, your body may even be contracted. While the perfected qualities are always present, in your experience they are not there; they are blocked. But if you open, joy is there; love is there. This is something we all should know. It should become part of the conventional wisdom of the person-on-the-street: joy (or any of the perfected qualities) can be experienced in this very moment for no reason. How many times have we had the passing thought, "Oh, if only I were twenty years younger," or "If only I had more money." Upon closer examination, we can see that these conditions—being younger or wealthier—do not guarantee happiness. Often people will see a photograph of themselves twenty years ago and think, "I really was nice-looking. But I didn't enjoy this about myself. I was constantly criticizing how I looked." There is no concrete cause that we can point to and say, "That always creates joy."

On the level of our conventional, everyday life, it is very helpful to become more familiar with the experience of being complete in this very moment. We would all be much happier in life if we applied this simple logic: "I am complete in this very moment!" We *can* begin to counter the logic of our habitual patterns of thinking. Every time you catch yourself bringing up a reason you are unhappy, just flash on the sun shining in the open sky, and remember your happiness has nothing to do with reasons. Think, "I am complete as I am in this very moment." Remind yourself that you do not want to become caught in the illusions of reasons. This can begin to support a shift toward trusting in a more fundamental experience of yourself while loosening the hold of your dependency upon illusions.

So what choice do you have? The choice is to be happy right now. And sometimes it works. Supported by that reasoning, you opened, and it worked. Shift your thinking, look clearly and directly into this very moment, and in five minutes you feel better. Why do you feel better? Because you do not allow the logic of conditions to continue. One definition of stupidity is continuing with logic that doesn't work. So we must recognize when we are applying that logic and interrupt it. Stop. The moment we stop, we begin to feel better. It is a very, very simple wisdom.

As described in the dzogchen teachings, spontaneously perfected qualities are already there. We don't create the qualities or produce them. But how directly you have access to these qualities is a different story. How much you can clear with *A* is the first step, the first development. How open you are will define how clearly you will experience spontaneous love, compassion, joy, and equanimity—the completeness of *OM*.

If you close your eyes and allow yourself to feel joy, it's there. You'll be surprised how easy it is to feel joy in your heart when you allow yourself to feel it. Often we don't allow the simple, direct experience of joy. "When he changes, then I'll feel happy." "When the kids are grown up, then I'll be peaceful." You have reasons, perhaps a whole list of them, and over time, this list of reasons doesn't get shorter. It gets longer and stronger until it is in bold letters and underlined. Think instead that positive qualities are already there, that they are fundamental to your being, and trust those qualities.

As we continue to practice the Five Warrior Syllables, there are positive signs or results that are traditionally described as "ordinary" results—results that are available in our everyday lives—and those described as "special" results, which are subtler and may be referred to as "meditative" results. Through practicing with *OM*, in our ordinary experience, our sense perceptions may be clear and vivid. The special result is the capacity to abide in clarity, which refers to the awareness of essence rather than of the object.

As a natural result of this practice, you will develop ceaseless confidence, a sense of completeness on a fundamental level. Ceaseless confidence is the term used to describe the experience that all the positive qualities are ceaselessly perfected in the unconditioned space of being. As you are, in this very moment, you are open, clear, and radiant with all positive qualities.

LISTEN TO TRACK 2
The Second Syllable: *OM*

CHAPTER
THREE

The Third Syllable: HUNG

Sing again and again the nondual sound of HUNG.
Radiate luminous blue light from the heart chakra.
The wisdom heat of the Four Immeasurables
Pervades like sunlight in all directions.
From nondual wisdom, allow the quality you need to radiate.
All distortions of doubt are overcome
And undeluded confidence is attained.
May I experience the wisdom of equanimity.

AS OUR MEDITATION practice progresses, we become increasingly familiar with openness. Through the vibration of *A*, we clear obstacles that obscure the open space of being, and we develop the capacity to trust that open space through abiding in the space that has opened up. We connect with our completeness and dissolve any sense of lack through the vibration of *OM*. Confidence develops in the clarity of the space as we abide in the vividness of each moment. Now we bring our attention to the heart. With our attention at the heart chakra, we discover that the open space of being and the light of our awareness are inseparable. According to the dzogchen teachings, the union, or inseparability, of openness and awareness spontaneously produces positive qualities. To express this in another way, when you feel complete, positive qualities spontaneously manifest. You are spontaneously happy when you feel complete. Things flow more easily in life when you feel complete. In the practice of the Five Warrior Syllables, when we activate the sound *HUNG* and focus at the heart, we are cultivating positive qualities by recognizing that they are already there.

As stated in the chapter on *OM*, space is not merely empty; its nature is compassion. In order to complete the journey of awakening, we must recognize the fullness of space. We must experience the boundless virtues that spontaneously arise. When we bring our attention to the heart, we develop a clear intention to experience positive qualities. There is a traditional four-line prayer that expresses the pure intentions of the Four Immeasurables. This prayer has been chanted by Buddhist practitioners for hundreds of years. The lines in the prayer express the pure intentions of love, compassion, joy, and equanimity, respectively. You may wish to say this prayer as a support for connecting with these four qualities.

May all sentient beings enjoy happiness and the cause of happiness.
May all sentient beings be free from suffering and the cause of suffering.
May all sentient beings not be separated from the great happiness devoid of suffering.
May all sentient beings dwell in the great equanimity free from the bias of
    happiness or suffering.

It is beautiful to connect with the pure intentions of the Four Immeasurables. And because we have cleared and connected with openness through singing *A*, and with awareness which pervades that space through singing *OM*, now from the inseparable union of space and awareness, the Four Immeasurables radiate without limit in all directions to all beings. But it is very important that we do not merely experience virtues as ideals that we aspire to. Therefore, as you bring your attention to your heart center, I encourage you to reflect upon the Four Immeasurables—love, compassion, joy, and equanimity—and discern which of these qualities is most needed or lacking in your everyday life. Perhaps you have been so goal-directed in your life that you have not taken the time to express kindness toward others or to take delight in their presence in your life, and so you wish to cultivate love. Perhaps you notice a general impatience and irritability toward your aging parents. Upon reflection, you recognize that you lack compassion in your relationship with them. Perhaps you are interested in healing a physical, emotional, or mental problem. When you reflect on the problem, you feel a total loss of joy in your life and so would like to focus on increasing your joy. Or you may find that you get caught up in appearances or are strongly affected by others' moods or opinions, and so you seek more balance and equanimity.

In the practice of the Five Warrior Syllables, having reflected upon your life, you draw attention to the heart chakra and sing *HUNG* again and again with the clear intention to feel one of the Four Immeasurables. Just bring the intention clearly to mind. Perhaps you think, "I want to feel joy in my heart." At this point in the practice, your clear intention is enough, because *HUNG* empowers that intention. As you sing *HUNG*, connect with the presence of the quality of joy. According to the highest teachings of dzogchen, the enlightened qualities are not developed but are already present in the clear and open space of being. Because you have felt open through *A* and complete through

OM, the quality of joy is present. We connect with the presence of this quality of joy—or whatever quality we need—as we sing *HUNG* again and again. And as we sing *HUNG*, whatever blocks or obstructs us from recognizing the presence of the positive quality is dissolved. Finally, we rest in the open and clear inner space supported by the presence of the quality, in this instance, supported by joy.

As you continue to open and deepen your experience of connecting with the quality of joy, it is important to free that joy from connection with any particular object. One of our problems is that we always need an object. If you tell people, "Be happy," they will say, "Give me one good reason to be happy." It is not easy to understand how to be happy without some particular reason. It is much easier for us to imagine having a problem. It seems to be problems rather than virtues that spontaneously and effortlessly arise! Everybody understands effortless doubts and spontaneous problems. We always seem to have some good reasons for doubt—intelligent, educated, and philosophically profound reasons. We think doubt is a sophisticated stance, but no matter how ornamented it is, the bottom line is that doubt interferes with the flow of one's life.

So we know about spontaneously arising doubt, but when we think about feeling joy, we always need an object; we always need some reason to be happy. Even then, we may become suspicious about the object of our joy, creating another opportunity to manifest doubt. In the practice of the Five Warrior Syllables, it is important to connect with the positive qualities of love, compassion, joy, and equanimity as unconditioned—without objects or reasons. Through the power of *HUNG*, we clear our doubts and hesitations to fully experience these positive qualities.

What is unique about the spontaneous qualities that arise from the union of openness and awareness is that they are not attached to particular objects.

The qualities are clear in their nature. I am not saying that they are just clear of doubts. I am saying that they are inherently clear. Usually when we say we feel "clear," we are saying that a problem was hard and we are finally free of it. "I think I have cleared it," or "I am ready to be free of it." You may be feeling clear, but your clarity is still in reference to the previously experienced problem.

Our concept of healing is often attached to a sense of problem. "I'm so happy that difficult project is done," or "I'm so happy that person finally left," or "I'm so happy I've been cancer-free for five years now." Our happiness is attached to reasons and conditions. The true power of healing minimizes the connection of healing to problems and maximizes the relationship of healing to the qualities that arise in the open and clear presence of being. The way you maximize these positive qualities is to have less dependence upon conditions. With joy, just feel joy without thinking of some object. "I'm just happy." Don't think about the project. Don't think about the person. Don't refer to the disease. Don't think about any problems. Imagine radiating the light of joy in that open, clear sky where nothing is missing, nothing is lacking, where everything is. That is how we cultivate a positive quality. In the practice of *HUNG*, we imagine a blue light radiating from the heart as we sing again and again the sound of *HUNG*. This light can support the experience of a positive quality without reasons and conditions. Then we rest, supported by the quality.

The word for meditation in Tibetan is *sgom*, which means "familiarity." We are simply not familiar enough with the spontaneous positive qualities of our nature. We glimpse joy or love for a moment. We feel it, but the next moment it is gone, and something else comes up to distract us. This is because of our lack of familiarity. If we are very familiar with openness and awareness, we are able to remain with the experiences that spontaneously arise for a longer period of time. Familiarity is important. Singing *HUNG* again and again supports us in developing familiarity with joyful experience or compassion or love or equanimity, without an object.

How much time do we spend thinking about our problems? "I'm struggling with this issue. I'm working on it. I can't believe I'm still doing this. I thought I was getting somewhere." We recite these thoughts like a mantra. Probably we recite fewer mantras and prayers than we do our negative self-talk. Our problems become very powerful because we meditate on them too long, too often, and in too much detail. There is very little space present in the mind when that mind is engaged in struggle. It is important to look back to a more fundamental place of being, either to a pure quality or to an open space.

There is a considerable amount of power related to where we focus our attention. Every time we dislike something and struggle with a situation, a person, our own health, or even our own identity, we focus on the negative. The experience is negative. We often continue in this way instead of finding another solution. We are trapped. "Why am I feeling this?" "Why is this person doing this?" We continue on and on. What's the point of repeating these thoughts? If we are saying a mantra, we repeat it to accumulate the positive result of that mantra. There is power in the accumulation. But repeating, "Why am I always doing this?" or "Why is this person always acting like this?" is not only asking the wrong questions, but continues to solidify a sense of problem, especially when we repeat them more than three times! Repeating the same question over and over is the result of the restlessness of no awareness and no solution. When we ask the same question again and again, we will find the wrong answer. Even if the question is a good one, if we are asking it from the wrong space, the result will not be good. In this practice of the Five Warrior Syllables, we are focusing on the space or focusing on the energy or focusing on one of the Four Immeasurable qualities. Focus on anything except the tired, negative pathway of your repetition of a problem. If you are able to do that, then positive changes are possible. A very common problem is not recognizing that we need to change our focus altogether.

Perhaps you have heard this familiar advice: "Let go. Just let go." There is wisdom in it. But perhaps you have not completely discovered that wisdom. When we say, "Let go," we usually focus on what is going rather than what is revealed when you let something go. By always focusing on the object or problem, the wisdom is not discovered; it is overlooked, and therefore it remains obscured.

So we come back to simply being. What could it mean to be? Don't think about a problem for the moment. Don't occupy yourself for this moment. Just get out of the familiar system of worry altogether. Breathe. Feel whatever is in this moment. If the sky is clear and the sun is shining, the only way to have a complete experience of this is if the mind is clear. Otherwise, no matter how beautiful the weather is, our internal experience is cloudy. You sit in the park on a beautiful, clear day with a completely cloudy mind. You are sitting on your karmic cushion, the very familiar, all too comfortable, habitual cushion of your habitual thoughts.

Remember how with *A* we spoke of connecting with the foundation of space? So "let go" simply means to find a space, a clear place in ourselves. Even a very tiny opening in the clouds of our discursive mind can be very powerful. Space is infinitely more powerful than the conditions that occupy us. Recognizing this and trusting this may take time, which is why we practice meditation. For all the time we spend focusing on problems—talking about them, thinking about them, feeling them—how much time do we actually spend with a sense of space or openness? The open space of our being becomes less and less available the more and more solid our issues become. But once we begin to connect with the space of our being, we have started a very powerful revolution.

Instead of thinking about a problem, feel directly in this moment your body, energy, and mind. Then focus on the heart chakra, and sing again and again the syllable *HUNG*. The vibration of *HUNG* penetrates conditions and patterns in this very moment. As they clear, as the space opens, you activate your intention to connect with one of the Four Immeasurables. The quality that you most need is already there; you are drawing your attention to it. Radiating blue light from the heart, you connect with the inseparable state of space and awareness and the power of love, compassion, joy, or equanimity. You connect, connect, connect, and you abide in that quality.

It is quite useful to think of the Four Immeasurables as doorways inward to our deepest essence and also as doorways outward through which we express virtue and goodness in the world. Through them we enter the center of our being, the union of openness and awareness. They support us to recognize and rest in the nature of being. This is the wisdom aspect. It is wisdom that cuts suffering. I often describe wisdom as openness. Openness is the sword that cuts ignorance, the root of suffering. Through the openness of our being, through the inseparable state of openness and awareness, we spontaneously express the qualities of enlightened energy in the world.

Are you happier when you rest in the inseparable state of space and awareness? Absolutely! You will be happier if you abide in this way. You connect with presence, potential, flow. You experience fewer blocks. Most of us would agree that joy is connected with the experience of freedom. The ultimate sense of freedom is a mind unbound by conditions. Most of us do not experience our mind unbound by conditions, or we do not recognize this open state. We usually only recognize freedom when a block we have experienced releases. The experience of feeling free is wonderful, because the flow that was previously blocked is now cleared.

Every time someone blocks your flow you suffer. The beauty of life is in the flow. I am using the word *flow* to refer to the inseparable state of emptiness and clarity. A traditional word to describe the experience of the inseparable state is *bliss.* When openness and awareness are there, we experience bliss; from this bliss, all positive qualities spontaneously manifest. This is referred to as spontaneous perfection: perfection that is already there.

In the inseparable state of space and light, the Four Immeasurables are spontaneously present. If we are practicing to connect with joy, we are seeking to minimize our reasons or conditions of joy. We are connecting with joy as an inner feeling, as a strong presence in the heart. At this point in the practice, we are not thinking of the expression of joy, which we will connect with later, so the experience of inner joy comes from the inseparable state of openness and awareness.

Human beings waste so much of life trying to be happy but looking in the wrong places. Where are we looking? First we look at our suffering and hate our suffering. We want to get out of it, and we look or wait for somebody or something to make us happy. We wait for some magic to happen, for some external causes and conditions to arrive. We spend so much time trying to be happy or put our hopes for happiness on some future event. This never works in any real sense.

How do we find genuine happiness? Go back to the source. Instead of looking out, look in. First clear the obstacles. Do not activate the obstacles further by thinking or analyzing. Work directly with body, energy, and mind. On the level of body, join movement with awareness. On the level of energy, work with prana, or subtle energy, by joining awareness and breathing. How do we work with mind? Observe directly, without elaboration and without following whatever arises. We don't plan the future, dwell on the past, or change the present. We leave it as it is. We abide. I am clearly not referring to the power of the analytical mind; I am talking about the power of awareness. Our awareness is not the product of thinking or analysis. Our awareness is our fundamental nature.

With *A*, our analogy was the clear, open sky of the desert. Our analogy with *OM* was the sunshine pervading that clear sky. Now, with *HUNG*, the analogy is the reflection of the sunlight. Light reflects on a variety of experiences. In the natural environment, light reflects on rocks, on water, on trees, on flowers. Internally, there is love or compassion or joy or equanimity. These qualities are a reflection of the space and the light. These qualities are pure.

The confidence that arises is undeluded confidence, the confidence that arises from the clarity and vividness of being. The wisdom of the inseparability of space and awareness is the wisdom of equanimity. Let's say you are looking at someone you love, or are listening to some music you appreciate. You just think, "Beautiful." Of course, you can attribute that experience of beauty to the person or the music, but it is also because of the space you are in.

When you truly enjoy someone or something, that means there is a good balance of space and light in your perception of that individual. You are open, which allows you to be happy. The more you attempt to grasp, hold onto, or control an experience you find enjoyable, the more suffering you will experience. But it is important to point out that when openness is there, it doesn't mean we are distant from our experience. It means the connection is there without the interference of our grasping mind. It is the balance of the connection and openness that gives rise to happiness. It is incorrect to say, "You make me happy." It is not "you." Because if it is "you" that makes me happy, then tomorrow you should make me happy, and the next day, no matter what else is going on, because you are the cause of my happiness. Clearly this logic does not work.

It is the space, the amount of openness and connection, that makes an experience beautiful. When you begin to lose that openness toward somebody, your happiness or joy diminishes, even though he or she is the same person with whom you were previously happy.

In ordinary experience, we refer to "the honeymoon period" of a love relationship. Your partner opens the door for you and pulls out your chair; you cook her favorite food; you bring him flowers. There are innumerable small gestures that arise spontaneously from the inspired openness we experience. Then it comes to the point where there is less and less of the opening of doors or pulling out of chairs, and eventually you find less and less to talk about. The sense of a free and open space is diminishing. Somehow that person now has the effect of occupying your space. You find yourself saying, "I just need some space." But what we usually mean by this is, "I need to get away from you so that I can be myself again." Why does that person have such an effect on us? Because we don't recognize the space in ourselves. We focus on the object or on what occupies us, rather than seek to clear, connect with, and recognize inner space.

As you begin to recognize this inner space, you are able to protect that space more. Your focus is not constantly caught up in the object. You find that external situations occupy or disturb you less and less. When an external situation occupies you less, there is more room for spontaneous connection. There is more and more room for life to be just as it is. Things have to change less and less to accommodate you to make you feel secure. I'm not saying it is easy, but the truth is there.

The special or meditative experience of *HUNG* will be abiding in the inseparable state of emptiness and clarity, which is experienced as bliss. The experience of *A*, the realization of emptiness, and the experience of

OM, the realization of luminosity or clarity, are inseparable. Emptiness and clarity are not separate. You cannot separate them. You are open; you are aware. You are aware; you are open. Abiding in that inseparable state of open awareness is blissful. Resting in that inseparable state of clarity and luminosity is abiding in the inseparable state, the nondual space. These are the three meditative experiences spoken of in dzogchen: emptiness, clarity, bliss. With *HUNG*, the meditative experience will be bliss.

The ordinary experience of *HUNG* will be a happy feeling. "I wonder what the weather is like today?" You open the window. "Wow!" You look up to the sky; the sun is shining; the clouds and rain of the past three days have cleared. That little bliss is the ordinary experience. You have an ordinary experience because the clouds are not there. Internally, your obscurations clear, and you feel a sense of space. In that space there is inner light. Because of that space and inner light, bliss is experienced. That bliss opens you up to love. When you feel happy, it is very easy to love. When you are not happy, it is harder to love. Even when you want to be loving, other negativities easily occupy that space. When you meet the wrong kind of circumstances, you can get agitated immediately and say unkind things to people you love.

I always give this example of a friend of mine who wished to have a more loving relationship with her mother. She realized that her mother was old, and she wanted to change her habitual pattern of being defensive and irritable with this woman she loved so much. Intellectually, she recognized this defensive pattern and wanted to change it. She thought about this and was determined to make a change. So she planned for a wonderful weekend visit with her mother, planning that they would go out for dinner and to a movie and just relax together and enjoy each other. On Friday afternoon, as she left her work and drove out of the city to the suburbs where her mother lives, she encountered lots of traffic. She had forgotten to bring her cell phone with her, so was unable to call her mother. She arrived late. Upon opening the door, her mother greeted her with, "You're late; you know how I worry," and then, "Oh, you look tired. Are you getting enough sleep? And what have you done to your hair? That isn't a new style is it?" That was just enough to awaken the old patterns in the daughter; her defensive irritation spontaneously manifested, and they were back in the same arguments.

My friend was not really engaging deeply enough in her meditation practice such that the change she desired could spontaneously manifest. Intellectually, she wished for it, but if she were to bring her focus to her heart and clear the obstacles to feeling love, perhaps her mother's comments would have been perceived in a different way. Perhaps she would have been able to laugh and reply, "Yes, my hair, so civilized all week, frequently gets a bit wild by Friday! I must be looking forward to going out with you tonight!" That is all it would have taken. If her practice had ripened in her, or touched her as deeply as her mother's comments did, she could have made that shift. At least she would not identify herself 100 percent as the target of her mother's comments.

So when we bring an intention to mind—in this case, the intention to cultivate love—we simply sing *HUNG* again and again, feeling the presence of love and radiating that feeling out in the form of blue light. We are not engaging in planning or thinking; we are simply opening our hearts to the experience of love.

Where does this experience of love come from? I'm repeating again: the luminosity and the space. When the obstacle or obscuration has cleared and created a space, we naturally experience some presence of light or awareness. In the union of the light and space, there is naturally some sense of bliss. That bliss becomes the seed for feeling love. It is as simple as that. It is as logical as that.

The power that *A, OM,* and *HUNG* refer to is a power that many people are unaware of. People often have no clue that connecting with and working from a deep inner source can support positive external change and transformation. In Tibet this process is not particularly articulated, because Tibetans do not care so much about external manifestation. In the Western world, on the other hand, we think it is very important, so much so that we are almost completely involved with external manifestation. But how much our external manifestations are affected by inner resources and views, and how consciously we access inner awareness, is another question.

We clear, open, recognize potentiality, and energize the potential with *A, OM, HUNG.* As we continue with the next warrior syllable, we seek to ripen this potentiality in order to manifest it for the benefit of self and others.

LISTEN TO TRACK 3
The Third Syllable: *HUNG*

CHAPTER
FOUR

The Fourth Syllable: RAM

Sing again and again the ripening sound of RAM.
Radiate luminous red light from the navel chakra.
All the enlightened qualities that one needs
Ripen like fruit in the warmth of the sun.
Meditating on these spontaneously arising virtues
The demons of conflicting emotions are overcome
And ripened confidence is attained.
May I experience discriminating-awareness wisdom.

RAM IS THE fourth warrior syllable. With *A* we have changeless body, *OM* is unceasing speech, *HUNG* is undeluded mind, and now with *RAM* we have ripened and perfected virtuous qualities. Bring your attention to the navel chakra as you sing *RAM* again and again. As you connect with the power of *RAM*, imagine that your obstacles are being burned and your virtuous qualities are ripening fully. With *RAM*, we continue the practice by bringing sanity and enlightened qualities into this world.

Sometimes we feel joy, but it does not find expression in our lives; we do not recognize the opportunity to bring this quality forth. Why do we need an inner quality to become concrete? In essence, it is not necessary; we are complete as we are, but we live in a world of conditions. In the relative world in which we live, it is important that our positive qualities find expression.

From the initial intention to cultivate one of the Four Immeasurables without object, you now feel the possibility of that quality coming into your relationship with your partner, your family, your work, or wherever it is needed. Bring to mind those places in your life where the quality you have connected with is needed. As you sing *RAM*, imagine that the quality is now radiating in the form of red light from your navel center. As you are radiating the light, send that love, compassion, joy, or equanimity to your relationships, to your workplace, to places of strife on this planet, wherever it is needed. You are sending it to places where it is lacking. What you connected with in your heart is now finding a very specific relation to something. It is ripening and becoming more concrete. Imagine or feel that the quality you experienced in your heart you now experience in the presence of others. Imagine the positive quality of love, compassion, joy, or equanimity radiating toward other people. Imagine others are positively affected by the radiance as sunlight ripens fruit. Imagine you are able to see those positive qualities reflected in others.

We began with space, awareness, and then the presence of an enlightened quality. For you, the particular quality—such as love, compassion, joy, or equanimity—may be present, but it is not necessarily ripened. *RAM* ripens it. When a positive quality ripens, it becomes substantial, external, functional. It becomes a story, involves interaction, and becomes something that can help somebody else. An actual manifestation comes from that ripened quality.

Having recognized the limitless potential of virtuous qualities with *OM* and energized a particular quality with *HUNG*, we now ripen that particular quality with *RAM* in order to manifest that quality in the world. There may be many potential virtuous qualities that we need to ripen in order to manifest them in life, whether in our professional life or in our relationships. Most of us would agree that we could be much kinder and more open in our relationships. By going back into ourselves and finding a clear inner space, we can open to others more.

In both *RAM* and the following syllable of action, *DZA*, it is useful to have conceptual awareness, like that of a monk or nun who has taken vows. For example, let's say you have taken a vow not to steal. You have completed a two-day fast, and you come upon food nicely laid out on a table. You are tempted to taste some of this food, even though it has not been offered to you. You think, "Should I? I'm so hungry. No, I have taken a vow not to steal, not to take what has not been offered." The conditions are such that you feel like you should go ahead. Your mindfulness says, "No, I took a vow." That kind of mind is very useful when we are cultivating love, compassion, joy, or equanimity. For example, when you are confronting a difficult person in your life, you know you come into areas of tension. You know he or she may say something that will affect you strongly. Simply by being mindful, you can shift things around. Mindfulness is helpful when a quality such as compassion has not ripened 100 percent. If a positive quality has ripened 100 percent, you don't need mindfulness anymore, because that positive quality is how you inherently *are*. When the compassion has not ripened, mindfulness is always helpful. A certain amount of effort is required to manifest the positive quality. In the

Vinaya, the body of teachings that contains the rules of behavior for monastic life, mindfulness serves most importantly. The Vinaya doesn't speak about spontaneous action; it speaks about vows of self-discipline.

At the level of manifestation, blocks and obstacles are more clearly visible. This has given rise to rules of conduct and laws in society. Human beings think that if we are not in control, the world will be a mess. This is not inherently true. What makes one cell become a heart and another become a lung? Nobody is behind the scenes, sitting on the fiftieth floor, planning all those things. Natural intelligence is inherent; spontaneous perfection is inherent. It is a question of accessing this in ourselves.

The wisdom connected with *RAM* is discriminating-awareness wisdom. When something is ripened, it has characteristics. It has a story. It is distinguishable or distinctive. Look at the colors and design of a single peacock feather. The metaphor with *RAM* is the sunlight ripening the fruit. When light shines on something, whatever the light touches ripens. When something ripens, it displays definite characteristics. One flower becomes blue; another becomes pink. These characteristics manifest out of the warmth of ripening. Personality emerges. Everything is not mixed into one mess; rather, detailed distinctive manifestation comes from that light, that heat. This is the power of *RAM*.

The confidence of *RAM* is ripened confidence. For example, you have confidence in the love you are feeling toward somebody. You are not hesitant to express your kindness toward another. You see more and more opportunities to manifest virtues in your life.

The power of *RAM* overcomes the demons of negative emotions. The demons of negative emotions refer to our inner demons of anger, jealousy, pride, attachment, and ignorance. When one's virtues of love, compassion, joy, and equanimity are ripened in their full details and characteristics, these demons are overcome.

The meditative experience of *RAM* is the burning fire of potentiality. When highly creative people walk into a new place, they can immediately recognize the possibilities there. They can recruit and mobilize resources. They are able to create because they come with potentiality. It is not that they come with all the tools and materials; they come with potentiality. The fire is there; that potent inner fire is there.

What is the distinction between an enlightened and an ordinary action? An enlightened action is not predetermined. You walk forth with internal bliss, and the positive quality spontaneously manifests for whoever needs it. That is called *enlightened* because it does not have any particular design or purpose. It manifests only when a need arises. It is not like the previous example of the woman driving on the highway, planning to love her mother for the weekend. Her action was not enlightened, because she had a very particular person in mind. She might have yelled when someone cut her off in traffic, even as she was planning not to yell at her mother. Of course, she ended up yelling at both the person driving in front of her and her mother. There is no enlightened quality in that. When there is an enlightened quality, this burning bliss is simply available; it is ready to come out. For an enlightened being, there is no need to manifest a quality. The circumstances are the only reason that it comes out. If there is a need for that quality to come out in order to help another person, it comes out.

So, what is enlightened quality? What is the most enlightened way of doing business? How can we be with each other in a more enlightened way? I think it is very simple. It is our experience; it is a sense of openness; we are not excluding but are including. Openness is wisdom, and wisdom must be present for any form of action to be compassionate. To the degree that wisdom and compassion are present, an action is more enlightened. If a relationship has wisdom and compassion, it is a more enlightened relationship.

The dzogchen teachings speak of enlightened beings manifesting in a variety of forms for the benefit of others. We can talk about peaceful, expansive, powerful, and wrathful manifestations. From a burning potentiality comes manifestation in a particular form, because sentient beings need that manifestation. Some people are benefited by a peaceful manifestation; some people need a more wrathful one. This does not mean that being peaceful doesn't work or being nice doesn't work. But the gesture of kindness is in relationship with others. It is about response. Need manifests, and you manifest the quality in response to the need, rather than approach a situation with an agenda of your own. I know a man who likes to hear people's problems. He will greet you with, "How are you?" If you respond, "I'm fine, and you?" he will press your hand into his, look into your eyes, and repeat, "How are you, really?" You can almost hear what kind of response to his question he would like to hear. It is as if he is saying, "Are you sure you are fine? Please tell me about your problems." He can actually make you feel a little sorry for yourself with that approach. His intention of asking, "How are you?" is actually to hear that you are not well so that he can take care of you. That is not enlightened!

Help seems more helpful if somebody comes to you asking for help, and you respond with support rather than arrive on the scene with the attitude, "I think you need my help." Sometimes when you are thinking, "You need my help," *you* are actually the one who needs help. So if the need is on your side, the response is not enlightened. Openness is lacking. When openness is lacking, wisdom is lacking. When wisdom is lacking, there is nothing enlightened about the desire to help. It becomes just another need.

It can be helpful to recognize when you are in that position, because you have the means, by singing *RAM*, to overcome your projections and open the space again for the natural and spontaneously arising enlightened qualities to emerge.

If you don't recognize your obstacles, you don't search for a means to overcome them. By singing *RAM* again and again, you clear your own agendas, ideas, and projections, and open yourself to be truly available for the needs of others.

The ordinary experience of *RAM* is a kind of restless enthusiasm or excitement. You are involved in a project that you are enjoying, and you stay up all night doing it. When I was a student in the Dialectic School at the monastery, there was quite a lot of excitement around study. As part of our training, we participated in vigorous philosophical debates late into the evening. One evening, a monk came back from debating, with his mind full of questions. He was so enthusiastic about the topic that even as he had his hand on the doorknob to enter his room, he stopped. Suddenly all these debating strategies came up in his mind. Before he had finished pursuing all his thoughts, morning came. He had remained at his door the whole night, just continuing his fantastic debate in his mind. When he had fully pursued all the discoveries he was making, he realized he had been standing at the doorway to his room for over five hours. By contrast, we know how hard it is when we are trying to do something that we don't really connect with. Just to sit down and spend two hours focusing on something until we finish can be hard. You may think it is important, but do you really feel it in your being? Is *RAM* really there? Is the burning fire really there? The ordinary *RAM* experience is like restless burning fire.

As love, compassion, joy, or equanimity ripens through *RAM*, and we increasingly feel the potency of the positive quality in our life, the manifestation of that quality is spontaneous and effortless.

LISTEN TO TRACK 4
The Fourth Syllable: *RAM*

CHAPTER
FIVE

The Fifth Syllable: DZA

Sing again and again the sound of action, the syllable DZA.
Radiate luminous green light from the secret chakra
To all beings who suffer and are in need.
Just as a good harvest satisfies hunger
The Four Immeasurables bring happiness and freedom.
External obstacles are overcome
And effortless confidence is attained.
May I experience all-accomplishing wisdom.

WE COME TO the final seed syllable, *DZA*, the seed syllable of action. *DZA* brings us to the place of manifestation. Let's say we have a project or job to do. We create a space and make time to do it. We gather resources, we summon our energy, we organize a plan, and then we do it. Throughout a lifetime, we will undoubtedly finish many projects in this manner. Sometimes we may thoroughly enjoy the process; sometimes we may find it difficult or unpleasant. Nevertheless, we will experience space, time, energy, action, and completion.

When we consider joy or another quality that is deeply personal or spiritual, we might have some kind of intention, but we probably don't have many resources or take action, and completion remains far away. That can change. With *DZA*, we set up the intention and clearly say, "This is my wish."

On a material level, we always have specific plans, specific things we want to accomplish in our lives. In a spiritual sense, what do you want to accomplish? I encourage you to have a goal. Set up a goal and have a clear plan.

We can always have good ideas about what we are going to do, but manifesting them is harder. When, through the practice of the Five Warrior Syllables, we find the courage to manifest, we feel so different. There is a sense of being sealed or confirmed. In our Western material world, this approach is very important. We value real action and positive change. We are not content to recite a mantra, thinking that in the next lifetime we will have some benefit. We want to see the changes faster than that. If you want to see the changes faster, you have to open internally; you have to bring the enlightened quality to life and feel it energetically. Then you have to manifest it.

If joy is the quality that you have cultivated, making a plan to manifest means saying, "I want to be joyful, and out of that, I want to bring some positive energy to my workplace. I want to clean up my desk, bring fresh flowers, and take time to greet the people around me every day." Recognize some changes you need to make in your workplace. Because you have cultivated some energy, those changes become possible. You embody that energy, so when you arrive at your place of work, the expression naturally and spontaneously comes out. In relationships, people talk about spending quality time together, and because of busy schedules, they often have to plan or schedule this quality time. Do this now. Reflect on the areas of your life into which you want to bring love, compassion, joy, or equanimity.

You may have had this intention many times before. Why is it any different this time? This time it is different because you have worked deeply inside yourself. You have opened yourself. You have cultivated some sense of deep connection with yourself. You have recognized some enlightened qualities that exist in you. You have become familiar with those qualities. They are there. They are active. They are ready to come forth. You are just recognizing the door through which manifestation will occur by saying, "This is the area in which I want the quality to manifest." This process works. But if you haven't done the previous work, the manifestation will not be there.

People often have no idea why they cannot bring about their good intentions, and conclude with a negative statement about their own defects and weaknesses. Or they feel they are a victim of others or of circumstances. The bottom line is that if the inner work is not done, the manifestation will not be there. Thinking alone does not work. You have to open, feel, connect, cultivate, and then allow something to manifest. If deep inside you are not open, if you really don't feel those positive qualities, or don't even realize those qualities exist in you, then how can you expect that positive qualities will manifest? If you are having a difficult relationship with your parents, and you are not opening and connecting with any positive qualities within yourself, how can you expect something positive to come out at the holiday dinner table? It doesn't work. Inner work needs to be done before you arrive at the table.

The fundamental principle of this practice is that no matter what you do in *DZA*, it is not going to work well unless you have some sense of *A*. This is often not understood. We struggle with manifestation. We can talk endlessly to ourselves, "Why do I get angry? Why did I do this again? What's wrong with me?" We can have the same conversation over and over, and nothing changes. We are not seeing anything good. In a way, asking why is tricky. Sometimes, we are not really looking for a solution. We are looking to blame. Or we find some kind of solution through a thinking process. We come to some conclusion, saying, "It's okay to have this problem. I am accepting myself; I'm accepting my limitations." Here, we come to some conceptual solution rather than a deeper nonconceptual sense of comfort. In order for you to have a deeper sense of healing, something deep inside needs to open. The struggle that occupies you needs to dissipate. Sing *DZA* again and again, releasing this sense of struggle and effort.

In human society, we typically live our lives with laws and vows and codes of ethics—from the military to the monastery, from household rules to governmental structures. But many times these structures are not a natural part of us. If society were more enlightened, the enforcement of laws would be minimal. There would be no use for regulations or enforcement, because people would feel these values internally rather than be forced to behave in a certain way.

The question to ask with *DZA* is whether you act from a clear and open space deep within yourself, or you do something because it is the "proper" thing to do. Some people live their lives following rules of propriety, and they are never truly touched by others, nor do they connect with their feelings in any real way. So the work that we are doing is going back to the source within. Can you see that? We are not simply thinking, "Oh, I need to love this person," and then talking to ourselves, discussing all the reasons it is not happening, and joining a support group for people who do not love enough. We need to go back. It seems that most of the encouragement in this practice is to go back. Go back into yourself and connect with an open and clear place, a place where the positive qualities are present; activate the presence in your body, emotions, and mind, and then allow the qualities to ripen. Having practiced in this way, you will naturally give birth to the expression of positive qualities in your life.

The spontaneous, effortless manifestation of enlightened beings is to help others. What exactly does that mean? *DZA* itself is effortless, spontaneous, enlightened activity. It is not the burning fire; it is activity itself. That is the *DZA*. In the special or meditative experience, enlightened beings manifest in a myriad of forms out of compassion, according to the needs of beings who are suffering. In our ordinary experience, it is as simple as that gesture of giving or a moment of expressing your love toward somebody. You express from your heart the words of your appreciation for somebody. Your heart is full. Your eyes are moist. Your gesture is spontaneous. That is a simple moment of virtuous activity.

I have a story that I would like to share, that illustrates the simple power of this practice in our everyday lives. I was teaching in Poland, where a group of us were practicing the Five Warrior Syllables for two days together. One of the participants just happened to be visiting the town where we were, as his stepmother was sick in the hospital nearby. They had had a cold relationship for over twenty years. He never felt loved by her, nor felt love for her. He always wanted to develop some sense of closeness, but it was a difficult situation. So he came to the retreat and was practicing, singing *A OM HUNG RAM DZA* again and again for the two days we were together. In the end, he told the story about what happened as a result of his practice. He said that deep inside he opened. His thoughts in the past were always, "Why doesn't she change so I can relate to her? If she would just once ask me something about myself." This is what we usually think, right? "If you change a little bit, then I can relate to you." Instead, he went deep inside through the practice and opened his heart. He opened his heart, felt some sense of the enlightened qualities in himself, and then said, "I'm going to take action." His action was a hug. He hugged his stepmother after twenty years of not touching. He said he felt the release of twenty years of energy in that hug. If not for the Five Warrior Syllables practice, he would not have been able to do it; he would not have even thought it was necessary to do. As it turned out, she passed away very soon after that.

When the causes and conditions ripen, *DZA* cannot be stopped. So when you sing this very forceful sound of *DZA*, focus on green light radiating from the secret chakra, located at the base of the central channel, approximately four finger-widths below the navel. Imagine that this light radiates to the areas in your life where you wish to see a positive effect. The wisdom connected with *DZA* is all-accomplishing wisdom. The accomplishment is there without effort. Look at all the unaccomplished areas of your life and consider how they came to be so. Perhaps the task takes too much energy, is too hard, is complicated, and occupies a territory in you that you don't even want to enter. If you have maintained the connection with *A*, then your *DZA* is a pure *DZA*. Reflect on the basic principles of this practice. It may even be a good model for business. If something is stuck, you don't push. You try to step backward and create a space—a space among the people involved, a space within the situation—and the moment that spaciousness is perceived, in that space more solutions will become apparent.

The confidence that you attain with *DZA* is effortless confidence, the confidence of spontaneity or confidence in effortlessness. This is not something that you pray for or that you develop. It is something that will come naturally as a result of your practice. If you practice, you will achieve this confidence.

LISTEN TO TRACK 5
The Fifth Syllable: *DZA*

CHAPTER
SIX

Establishing a Daily Practice

NOW THAT YOU have been introduced to the Five Warrior Syllables practice, I encourage you to explore it as a daily practice. As I mentioned in the Introduction, this is a practice that can change your life. In order to bring this practice directly into your day-to-day experience, as you begin each practice session, reflect upon a problem that exists in your life that you would like to change. Then decide to cultivate an antidote for the obstacle, block, or obscuration that you wish to clear. For instance, you may notice that you express irritation with your family and criticize them. You may wish to cultivate love, the antidote for anger. Compassion is an antidote for a self-centered view of the world, joy can be an antidote for depression, and equanimity is an antidote for emotional volatility or unclear boundaries in your relationships.

Before you begin a session of practice, you may wish to perform the tsa lung exercises, which are described in the Appendix. These help you to create a clear and strong focus in each chakra and are powerful exercises that clear obstacles to abiding in openness.

Remember that each of the syllables connects with a basic principle. *A* clears and connects you with openness. *OM* supports awareness, the feeling of completeness in that openness, and the spontaneous presence of all virtuous qualities. With *HUNG*, you connect with a particular enlightened quality that you need in your life—such as love, compassion, joy, or equanimity—a quality that comes from the inseparability of openness and awareness. *RAM* ripens that quality and brings it into your relationships. With *DZA*, you spontaneously and effortlessly manifest that quality wherever it is needed.

Through practicing with the CD, you can become familiar with the simple sounds that bring you to a state of abiding in the nature of mind. When you begin the practice of the Five Warrior Syllables on your own, I encourage you to emphasize what you connect with first. Perhaps, as you begin your practice, you seek to develop familiarity simply with the sense of bringing your awareness to the particular chakra and feeling the vibration of the sound as you sing the syllables. Perhaps you find you are able to connect with the images of the metaphors for each of the syllables. If so, your practice may consist of singing *A* while imagining and feeling the clear, open desert sky and then resting there; singing *OM*, you imagine the sunlight radiating in that sky; singing *HUNG*, you imagine light radiating and reflecting on objects in the natural world; with *RAM*, you imagine the light ripening nutritious fruits and grains; and with *DZA*, you imagine the fruits and grains feeding those who are hungry and in need. Or you may feel a connection with the radiance of the colored light as you sing each syllable. With *A*, you radiate white light from the forehead chakra; with *OM*, you radiate red light from the throat; with *HUNG*, you radiate blue light from the heart chakra; with *RAM*, you radiate red light from the navel chakra; and with *DZA*, you radiate green light from the secret chakra. As you develop more familiarity with the practice, you can gradually include the meanings of the syllables and their sacred qualities. It is important to abide in the space that opens up within you after singing each syllable.

I also encourage students to bring the qualities they are cultivating into expression in everyday life. As you rise from your meditation each day, do not leave the practice on your cushion or in your shrine room. If you have been cultivating love, express that love with some gesture during the day. Do not simply engender loving thoughts about others; express those thoughts. Send an e-mail; write a postcard; make a phone call.

THE THREE EXCELLENCES

Before you begin any practice session of meditation, even if you sing the warrior syllables in your car as you drive to work, it is important to develop the strong and clear intention to attain realization in your practice so that you may benefit others. This is the first excellence. Then, when you actually engage the practice, connect with openness and awareness as your natural state. This is your main practice and the second excellence. Finally, at the conclusion of your practice, it is important to dedicate the merit of the practice to all beings. Pray that whatever benefit you have received from your practice becomes available for all others who suffer. Arouse genuine feeling by thinking of specific people in your life who you know are in need. Praying sincerely from your heart in this way, the positive benefits of your practice are greatly multiplied, are sealed, and can't be lost. Keep these three excellences in mind.

POSTURE

When practicing the Five Warrior Syllables meditation, I recommend that you sit on a cushion on the floor in what is known as the five-point meditation posture: cross-legged, spine straight and chest open, hands in equipoise position (palms facing up, left palm resting on right, placed low on the belly, about four finger-widths below the navel), jaw tucked slightly down and in to lengthen the back of the neck, and the eyes lowered. The gaze of the eyes follows the line of the nose.

You may close your eyes while singing each syllable. When abiding after singing each syllable, I recommend that the eyes remain open and rest in the space before you. If you find that this is too distracting, you may close your eyes.

If you are unable to sit on a cushion on the floor, you may sit in a chair with your feet flat on the floor and your back upright and free of the support of the chair.

THE PRACTICE

On the CD that accompanies this book, I guide a practice of the Five Warrior Syllables. Tracks One through Five are short meditations, one for each syllable. Track Six is a guided meditation of the full practice of all the five syllables together. If you have read, reflected, and then listened to the tracks corresponding to the syllables individually, and have gained some familiarity with them, I recommend practicing with the full guided instructions on Track Six. I am including guided instructions for the complete practice similar to what you will hear on the CD, with some additional suggestions.

> Relax your body, breath, and mind. Connect with this moment, here and now. Create a clear, heartfelt intention to obtain healing and benefit from this practice not only for yourself but for others. Next, bring to mind a condition that you wish to transform. As you bring

this to mind, feel directly and intimately how you experience this condition in your body, energy, and mind. Know that what obscures or troubles you now will become a doorway to a greater opening, will become part of your path to achieve liberation for the benefit of all.

Gradually draw your attention to the third eye, to the forehead chakra. As you sing the primordial sound *A*, imagine and feel that the vibration and healing power of *A* dissipates and releases blocks of the body, emotions, and obscurations of mind. Continuously sing the sound *A*, and imagine and feel that the vibration of this sound *A* dissipates negative emotions and clears whatever discomfort you may be experiencing in this very moment. Without judging your feelings or sensations, continuously sing *A*. Radiate white light from the forehead chakra as you sing. Gradually feel a deeper and deeper connection to the sound.

A … A … A …

Continuously sing *A* as you connect with inner space, like the open expanse of a desert with a crystal clear sky. Imagine your thoughts dissipate into the crystal clear sky. Feel this inner space. In this way, you overcome deep fears and experience trust and confidence in openness, in the space you are feeling at this very moment.

A … A … A …

Rest and connect with this openness within yourself. Abide in openness without changing or elaborating anything.

Gradually draw your attention to your throat, and imagine and feel this deep openness with no obstacles. Feel confidence in that space of openness. Feel completeness in that space of openness. There is nothing lacking at this very moment in your life. Inner essence is complete with all positive qualities, with no external reasons or causes. Like images in a mirror, all experience is clearly reflected. Connect with this sense of completeness as you sing the sacred sound *OM*. Keep your attention at the throat and radiate red light as you sing *OM* again and again.

OM … OM … OM …

Deep inside, feel a sense of completeness. Nothing is lacking; nothing is missing. Feel the luminous quality of awareness in that openness. Feel the sun shining in that clear desert sky. You are fully present and aware in that openness.

OM … OM … OM …

Abide: open, aware, complete.

Gradually draw the attention to the heart chakra. Feel clear openness in the heart chakra. Sing the sacred sound *HUNG* again and again, and allow the sound to help you to connect deeper and deeper. As you feel a deep sense of openness in the heart chakra, imagine the presence of the Four Immeasurables: love, compassion, joy, and equanimity. Bring to mind a clear intention to experience one of these qualities. Feel it strongly and deeply as you continuously sing the sacred sound. Feel the heat of the quality. This is inner quality, with no conditions or reasons. Feel the quality becoming stronger and more vivid and alive in your heart as you radiate blue light. Sing this sacred sound *HUNG* again and again.

HUNG ... HUNG ... HUNG ...

Continuously feel the quality in the open space of your heart. Feel it through your body, through your skin, through your breath. Feel the quality emanating from you, radiating like the sunlight radiating in the clear and open sky. Feel the quality radiating, free of judgment and the conceptual mind. Allow it to flow as you continuously sing:

HUNG ... HUNG ... HUNG ...

Abide, supported by the quality.

Gradually draw your attention to the navel chakra. As you sing the warrior seed syllable *RAM*, imagine and feel the quality of fire that activates and ripens the positive quality you felt and cultivated in the heart. Feel this quality increasing with the fire and energy of the sacred sound *RAM*. Feel the quality as it intensifies and is empowered with the sound *RAM*. The sound *RAM* ripens that quality and defeats the negative emotions. As you sing the sound *RAM*, imagine the positive quality is radiating out into the world, wherever the quality is needed.

RAM ... RAM ... RAM ...

The quality ripens through the power of the sound *RAM,* as sunlight ripens the fruit. Radiate the red light of the positive quality to benefit your place of work, your relationships, your home. Radiate the fire light of the ripened quality to different places in your life until you see some shifts and changes.

RAM ... RAM ... RAM ...

Abide with the experience of ripeness.

Gradually draw your attention to the secret chakra at the base of the central channel. Imagine and feel a strong manifesting quality as you sing the sacred sound *DZA*, the sound of action, the sound of spontaneous, effortless action. Feel the ripened quality fully and spontaneously manifesting when it meets the right circumstances. The sound *DZA* helps you to manifest this quality without any effort. You naturally experience the positive quality in your relationships; you naturally discover the quality in your home. Continuously sing *DZA*. The fruit has ripened and is enjoyed. The positive quality manifests in your life and benefits others.

DZA ... DZA ... DZA ...

Continuously feel the spontaneous manifestation, radiating green light from the secret chakra. Feel the vibration of *DZA* clearing obstacles to spontaneous manifestation.

DZA ... DZA ... DZA ...

Rest in effortless confidence.

Appendix: Clearing Obstacles
with the Tsa Lung Exercises

IN ORDER TO promote the release of physical, energetic, and mental obstacles, I recommend the practice of the five tsa lung exercises. These exercises are very powerful and can be done before you begin the practice of the Five Warrior Syllables. I will describe the practice of these five exercises. They are also presented in detail in my book *Healing with Form, Energy, and Light.* In Tibetan, *tsa* means "channel" and *lung* means "vital breath" or "wind." Through bringing the focus of the mind, the breath, and the physical movements together, in each exercise we seek to open particular chakras, or energetic centers, in the body and clear the obstacles that disturb and obscure us from recognizing the pure and open space of being.

THE THREE MAIN CHANNELS

When working to clear obstacles through the tsa lung exercises, imagine the three main channels of the body: the central channel and two secondary channels. These channels are made of light. The central blue channel rises straight through the center of the body and widens slightly from the heart to its opening at the crown of the head. It is described as being the diameter of a bamboo arrow. The side or secondary channels, one red and one white, are somewhat smaller in diameter and join the central channel at its base, about four finger-widths below the navel. The side channels rise straight up the body from this junction, paralleling either side of the central channel. Whereas the central channel rises straight through the crown, the side channels curve around under the skull, passing down behind the eyes, and open, one at each nostril. The right channel is white, representing method (skillful means) or qualities. This is the channel of the male energies. The left channel is red and represents wisdom. It is the channel of the female energies.

The chakras along the central channel have different qualities and characteristics and present different opportunities for the meditator. The central channel is the path for us. It is not a physical road or highway, but is a path, a stream of consciousness. If you feel clear, clear is a state of mind. Feeling complete is a state of mind. Feeling the presence of the positive qualities is a state of mind. Feeling a ripening state of the qualities is a state of mind. Manifesting is a state of mind. So while it is mind, mind, mind, mind, mind, each is the foundation for the next level, and that is called path.

I joke sometimes, saying that if you love someone very much, you should say, "I love you from my central channel." That is better than loving someone from the heart, because when you say "from my heart," you may simply be referring to your emotions. The central channel is the clear and open expression of the totality of your being.

In experience, it is hard to define the central channel. There is no ordinary terminology for it. The simple expression would be to say it is some deep sense of settling in oneself, completely resting with full awareness rather than resting by sleeping. We all know how to rest by sleeping deeply, but to rest with full awareness is not something everyone knows how to do. The tsa lung exercises are useful to remove the blocks and obstacles to resting deeply with full awareness.

EXERCISING THE PATHWAYS OF THE SECONDARY CHANNELS

There is a simple exercise you can do to train the focus of the mind and the breath together and to begin to familiarize yourself with the presence of these channels of light. Inhale, feeling pure, nourishing air coming into your body through your nostrils. Imagine that the breath follows the path of the red and white side channels to the junction four finger-widths below the navel. Hold the breath slightly here, keeping the focus at this junction. To emphasize the hold, pull up slightly on the muscles of the pelvic platform, anus, and perineum. Then, in a slow and controlled way, release the breath and relax the hold. As the breath slowly releases, follow the pathway up the body through the secondary channels and out through the nostrils. Feel this releasing breath carrying blocks and obstacles from the body, energy, and mind. Imagine that these obstacles dissolve instantly in the vast surrounding space. Repeat, inhaling fresh and clear air that nourishes and supports your concentration, following the pathway of the secondary channels down to the junction, holding slightly and maintaining the focus at the junction while pulling upward as described before, then releasing the breath, and as you slowly exhale through the nostrils, following the pathway of the secondary channels up through the body.

At first, you can practice for a total of twenty-one continuous breaths and then rest, simply abiding in the moment in an uncontrived way for as long as the experience is fresh. Eventually, you may wish to build up until you can comfortably do 108 repetitions of this breath. In this way, you can become more stable and familiar with the pathways of the channels and the principle of releasing. You also train your focus to become calm and clear. In this preliminary exercise, we are not actively engaging the vital breath, or prana, in the central channel, except to be aware of the presence of this channel.

THE FIVE TSA LUNG EXERCISES

In each of the five exercises, there are four stages to the breath: inhaling, holding, re-inhaling, and exhaling. In each exercise, you inhale through the nose and imagine the breath follows the pathway of the side channels until it reaches the junction as described earlier. When the air reaches the junction just below the navel, the energies of the two side channels, male and female, unite and move up the central channel. Imagine that the central channel fills with positive energy that rises to the chakra where you are working in the particular exercise. The breath is held throughout this process, and the focus is held at the particular chakra.

While holding the breath at the chakra specified in each exercise, the positive quality of the prana is held as a vessel holds nectar. Then, without exhaling, you inhale again, taking in a bit more pure air, and continue to hold the breath throughout the movement. This re-inhalation increases the heat and energy that supports the spreading of the prana like nectar throughout the body. The main concentration of this spreading prana is at the chakra specified in each exercise. At the end of the movement, the exhalation descends the central channel and moves out through the side channels and nostrils. Think that this exhalation exhausts, expels, and clears the blocks and obstacles that would obscure your natural awareness. Imagine that the chakra itself opens and clears and supports the experience of open awareness at that chakra. At this point, the breath returns to whatever breath is normal for you, as you rest in open awareness.

When performing the tsa lung, it is recommended that you repeat each exercise at least three times. These exercises can clear gross obstacles such as those that cause disease or strong negative emotions, clear or exhaust the momentum that drives obscuring thoughts, and clear obstacles that disturb your ability to recognize and rest in your own natural mind.

At the end of the set of three, simply rest with attention at the chakra you have been working with, opening and relaxing as the physical, and then the energetic, energies settle. Rest your mind in the open space hosted by the chakra as long as the experience remains fresh and uncontrived. If you can rest with your eyes open, that is best. If, in keeping your eyes open, you find you become distracted, simply close your eyes.

1. Upward-Moving Tsa Lung Exercise

The upward-moving tsa lung exercise opens the throat, forehead, and crown chakras. Inhale through the side channels and imagine that pure air enters and fills the central channel up to the throat chakra. Hold the breath, concentrating the focus at that chakra. Re-inhale and continue to hold and maintain the focus. Feel the prana spreading upward internally, nurturing all the sense organs located in the head. Bring to mind the obstacles you seek to clear or exhaust. Slowly start rotating the head five times counterclockwise. Feel the prana moving upward through your head in a spiral movement. Then reverse directions and rotate the head five times clockwise, continuing the same feeling of the nectar spreading upward in a spiral movement, as if washing and cleansing all that it touches. At the end of the movement, exhale the air.

Imagine that the breath descends the central channel and obstacles leave the body through the nostrils via the side channels. Your attention is directed upward as you exhale, as you imagine that the obstacles carried by the prana are expelled through the crown chakra. Repeat the exercise a total of three times. With each repetition, the exhalation releases and clears obstacles. After the third repetition, rest your mind in open awareness, feeling the throat, forehead, and crown chakras open and clear. Your eyes may be either open or closed at this point. Rest in open awareness as long as the experience remains fresh and uncontrived.

NOTE: The instructions are to hold the breath throughout each exercise and exhale only at the end. However, if you feel you need more air before the movement is completed, do a short re-inhalation. If that is not enough air, repeat a movement only three instead of five times, building up your stamina over time until you are able to do five.

2. Life-Force Tsa Lung Exercise

The life-force tsa lung exercise opens the heart chakra. Inhale through the nostrils, following the pathway of the side channels, imagining that the breath enters the central channel at the junction and rises up to the heart. Hold the air at the chest level, concentrating at the heart chakra. Re-inhale, holding and maintaining the focus at the heart chakra while feeling the prana spread internally through your chest, nurturing the area of your heart. You might feel or sense the obstacles you are seeking to exhaust and clear. Extend your right arm straight out from your body and rotate the arm five times overhead in a counterclockwise direction, making a motion like a lasso. Feel the vital air expanding your chest and your life force being strengthened. Then extend and rotate the left arm five times clockwise with the same lasso motion. Still maintaining the breath retention and the focus, place your hands on your hips and rotate the upper torso five times toward the right and then five times toward the left. At the end, exhale the breath, imagining that it descends through the central channel and ascends through the side channels, releasing through the nostrils. Feel the obstacles being released and exhausted with the exhalation. Imagine the heart chakra opening and releasing as well. Repeat this exercise a total of three times. At the end, rest in open awareness with your focus hosted or supported by the opening at the heart chakra. Remain for as long as the experience is fresh and uncontrived.

3. Fire-Like Tsa Lung Exercise

The fire-like tsa lung exercise opens the navel chakra. Inhale the pure air through the nostrils, following the pathway of the side channels, and bring the prana to the junction where it enters the central channel and moves up to the navel. Hold the air with the *vase retention*. Vase retention (Tibetan: *bar lung*; Sanskrit: *kumbhaka*) refers to the act of pulling up the muscles of the anus, perineum, and pelvic platform, creating a basket, while the diaphragm pushes down to create a lid. Take care not to hold with too much pressure or tension. Concentrate your mind at the navel chakra within the "vase." Re-inhale, maintaining the focus and the vase retention. Imagine that the prana spreads, filling the vase and nurturing the navel area. Rotate the abdomen five times counterclockwise, maintaining the concentration and the vase retention, as well as bringing to mind any obstacles you are clearing. Then rotate five times in a clockwise direction. At the end of the movement, the exhalation moves down through the central channel and out the side channels through both nostrils. Feel the obstacles releasing through your breath and dissolving into space. Feel the opening and release at the navel chakra. Repeat the exercise a total of three times. Then rest in open awareness with your focus hosted by the navel chakra. Rest as long as the experience remains fresh and uncontrived.

4. Pervasive Tsa Lung Exercise

The focus of the pervasive tsa lung exercise begins at the junction of the three channels, moves throughout the central channel, pervades the entire body, and then spreads beyond the bounds of the body. Inhale pure air through the side channels to the junction, bringing the prana into the central channel and holding the focus and breath there. Imagine that the prana begins to spread throughout the entire body. Re-inhale, feeling the vital breath spreading and particularly pervading those places where the energy seems blocked. As you feel the spread of the vital breath throughout your body, raise your hands above your head. Clap them together sharply above the top of your head and rub your hands together, generating a sense of heat and energy. Continuing to hold the breath, massage your whole body, particularly those areas where you experience any injuries or blockages. Feel these areas come alive, as if every cell of your body were vibrating with vital breath. Still holding the breath, perform a movement similar to shooting an arrow, opening the upper torso. Do this five times to the right and then five to the left. At the end, as you exhale, prana descends the central channel and the obstacles are expelled through the nostrils via the side channels. Experience release through all the pores of your body. Let your breath return to normal, and then repeat the exercise for a total of three times. At the conclusion, rest in open awareness. Your focus can be hosted by the chakra at the junction of the three channels. Rest as long as the experience remains fresh and uncontrived.

5. Downward-Moving Tsa Lung Exercise

The downward-moving tsa lung exercise opens the secret chakra. In a seated position, cross the legs at the ankles, with the right leg in front of the left and the knees separated and up off the ground. Place each hand on the outside of the corresponding knee to form a stable base of support. Inhale through the nostrils and follow the pathway of the side channels. At the base of the central channel is the secret chakra. Concentrate the attention and the prana at the secret chakra and create a "basket hold" by pulling up on the muscles of the anus, perineum, and pelvic floor. Re-inhale, letting the prana spread and imagining that the area of the secret chakra is being nurtured. Turn your upper body toward your right knee and grasp that knee with both hands, using the knee as a stable support while you rotate your hips five times counterclockwise. Next, turn toward the left knee and grasp that knee with both hands, using it as a stable support while you rotate the hips five times in a clockwise direction. Bring the body back to the center and, grasping both knees, rotate the hips five times in a counterclockwise direction and then five times in a clockwise direction. Throughout the movements, the breath is held and the basket hold is maintained. Your focus remains at the secret chakra as you work to exhaust and clear obstacles. At the end of the movement, exhale, imagining that obstacles are carried on the prana as it moves through the side channels and releases through the nostrils, dissolving into space. Imagine that the subtle prana moves in a downward direction as the secret chakra releases and opens. Repeat the exercise a total of three times.

On your final repetition, remain for a longer time in the state of contemplation, experiencing the changes at the levels of the body, energy, and mind. Rest deeply in open, uncontrived awareness as long as the experience remains fresh.

Acknowledgments

FOR THE PAST thirty-three years, my teacher, Yongdzin Tenzin Namdak Rinpoche, has been a perpetual inspiration and compassionate guide. His support and counsel help me to clarify the ancient Bön teachings as medicine for modern times. I wish to express my one-pointed devotion to him and deep appreciation for his wisdom and kindness. In preparation for this book, he afforded me precious time in Nepal and France, where we discussed this presentation of the Five Warrior Syllables practice. I would also like to thank both Khenpo Tenpa Yungdrung Rinpoche and Ponlop Trinley Nyima Rinpoche for the time and attention they brought to this discussion.

Most important, I wish to extend my heartfelt thanks to Marcy Vaughn, a close and senior student. Marcy worked for many hours to make this book on the Five Warrior Syllables accessible to a Western audience. Personally, it has been wonderful working with her, and without her this book would not have been possible.

Over the past fifteen years, many of my students from sanghas around the world have accepted positions of administrative responsibility to support the growth of my teaching and practice centers. I want to acknowledge their invaluable help, as it frees me to concentrate on teaching.

I would also like to thank Tami Simon, president of Sounds True, for her interest in publishing this audio book. I thank her team at Sounds True: Kelly Notaras, Chantal Pierrat, Chad Morgan, Mitchell Clute, and Haven Iverson. All have brought care and talent to this project.

Finally, as I travel throughout the world to teach and guide students, I am grateful for the love of my wife, Tsering Wangmo. Her patience when I am away for considerable lengths of time and her understanding of my work reinforce my efforts on behalf of all sentient beings.

Tenzin Wangyal Rinpoche
Paris, France
August 2006

About the Author

TENZIN WANGYAL RINPOCHE, the founder and resident teacher of Ligmincha Institute in Virginia, was one of the first lamas to bring the Bön Dzogchen teachings to the West. Tenzin Rinpoche lived and studied with Tibetan masters of Bön Buddhism from the age of 13 until completing an eleven-year course of traditional studies at the Bönpo Monastic Center, Dolanji, HP, India. Rinpoche received scholarships from the University of Oslo, Norway, and Lund University, Sweden, and held the position of Rockefeller Fellow at Rice University. He is the recipient of a National Endowment for the Humanities grant, and is the author of several books: *Healing with Form, Energy, and Light: The Five Elements in Tibetan Shamanism, Tantra, and Dzogchen; Wonders of the Natural Mind; The Tibetan Yogas of Dream and Sleep;* and *Unbounded Wholeness.* Rinpoche currently resides in Charlottesville, Virginia, with his wife and son, and travels and teaches throughout Europe, the United States, and Mexico, where he has founded over thirty centers for the study and practice of Bön Buddhist meditation.

For further information about the teaching schedule of Tenzin Wangyal Rinpoche, contact:

Ligmincha Institute
313 2nd Street SE, Suite 207
Charlottesville, VA 22902
(434) 977-6161
www.ligmincha.org
ligmincha@aol.com

About Sounds True

SOUNDS TRUE WAS founded with a clear vision: to disseminate spiritual wisdom. Located in Boulder, Colorado, Sounds True publishes teaching programs that are designed to educate, uplift, and inspire. With more than 600 titles available, we work with many of the leading spiritual teachers, thinkers, healers, and visionary artists of our time.

To receive a free catalog of wisdom teachings for the inner life, visit www.soundstrue.com, call toll-free 800-333-9185, or write: The Sounds True Catalog, PO Box 8010, Boulder CO 80306.

SOUNDS TRUE
awakening wisdom

CD SESSIONS